Merry Christmas,
Happy New Year,
and Welcome Home!

Joy

1963

RODIN

BY ALBERT E. ELSEN

THE MUSEUM OF MODERN ART, NEW YORK

Distributed by Doubleday & Co., Inc., Garden City, New York

Published by The Museum of Modern Art, 1963
11 West 53 Street, New York 19, New York
All rights reserved
Library of Congress Card No. 63–14847
Designed by Susan Draper
Printed in the Netherlands by Joh. Enschedé en Zonen, Haarlem

HOMAGE

Cézanne said that a painting is a theory that has been realized. One could say the same thing about sculpture in general, but not about Rodin's sculpture. Rodin is a tempest, an explosion. All the theories are toppled, only the complexity of living persists with this instinctive thirst for procreation.

That's also why the young man—almost an infant—that I was when I arrived in Paris could neither understand nor grasp the immense chaotic richness which Rodin's œuvre embodies. Despite my effort to explain to myself that at that moment I could neither comprehend nor love Rodin, I cannot rid myself of a kind of guilt complex toward him. Imagine, I never approached him; and I could have done so on many occasions. On the contrary, I fled from him. I remember a story which even today makes me blush with shame. In 1912, at the Salon National des Beaux-Arts of which Rodin was president, I exhibited two heads that I had made in 1911—one in bronze, the other in plaster. My friend the sculptor Léon Cladel (brother of Judith Cladel, Rodin's secretary), was asked that year to receive the President during his visit to the opening. Naturally I ran away during this occasion. Returning after the presidential visit, I saw my friend Cladel running toward me, all flushed with the excitement of bringing me what he thought was good news. "Rodin," he told me, "has noticed your little bronze head, and he asked me to tell you that if you work hard, something will become of you."

Incredible as it must seem, this news made me deadly sad. I asked myself, "What could be so wrong with my little sculpture that Rodin liked it?" For a long time, this idea did not leave me.

It was only during the First World War, or maybe just after—I don't remember the exact date too well—that I could visit the Musée Rodin. My joy was immense, and so was my enthusiasm at finding so many riches piled up. And "piled up" is the right expression for it. Among other things, I was struck by a certain aspect of some of his sculptures. Probably influenced by the sculptures from his collection of ancient art, he had created what might be called "torsos." These figures without arms, heads and legs were endowed with a sense of mystery, and one needed imagination to complete the figure. I did not want to make "torsos," but at that moment I understood that a work of art needs the element of mystery. I clearly saw that what Rodin was doing instinctively was not so different from what we, the Cubists, were doing in a more intellectual way, and that at certain points it was even more complex. And he had created an immortal work—The Gates of Hell. If I may say so, he was more advanced than we. And his sculpture had a skin, while ours at that epoch was still quite raw. It seems to me that he surpassed anything done in his time, either in painting or sculpture.

I don't want to end these few words without paying homage to the memory of Curt Valentin, who did so much for the re-evaluation of Rodin in this country.

Hastings-on-Hudson, New York, November 1962   JACQUES LIPCHITZ

ACKNOWLEDGMENTS

Although this book is a result of studies on Rodin begun more than a dozen years ago, it is the immediate outcome of a most welcome invitation extended on behalf of the Trustees of The Museum of Modern Art to prepare a monograph to be published concurrently with the major exhibition of Rodin's work being presented jointly by the Museum and The California Palace of the Legion of Honor. Through the generosity of a grant by the Clark Foundation to the Indiana University Foundation, it was possible to undertake important research in Paris during the summer of 1962 and there study at first hand many of the best casts of Rodin's sculpture. Mme Cécile Goldscheider, Curator of the Musée Rodin, who in recent years has organized many exhibitions in France and abroad that have greatly furthered the growing appreciation of Rodin's work, made available certain of that museum's files of newspaper clippings and also provided many of the photographs reproduced in this book. During my sojourn in Paris, I received helpful advice from Miss Darthea Speyer and Mme Hélène Baltrusaitis of the Centre Culturel Américain; Claude Bernard Heim of the Galerie Claude-Bernard; Jean de Ruaz; Mme Dina Vierny; and Professor William Homer of Princeton University. Special thanks must go to Wayne V. Andersen, who has taken much time from his own researches in order to expedite the obtaining of additional material and information required from Paris.

I have received constant stimulus and encouragement from many others with a particular interest in Rodin. Especially welcome were Leo Steinberg's provocative questions and sharing of insights; Margaret Scolari Barr's comments on the relationship between Rodin and Medardo Rosso (to be dealt with in her forthcoming monograph on the latter artist); and the kindness of Jacques Lipchitz, who by writing his own "Homage" to Rodin has provided the most suitable of forewords. Special mention should be made of the unselfish assistance of Charles and Regina Slatkin in locating for me little-known works of Rodin that they had uncovered while preparing their own exhibition on the sculptor. I am grateful both to Captain Edward Steichen, for his enthusiasm for this undertaking and the superb photographs of Rodin and his sculpture which he has made available, and to John Szarkowski, his successor as Director of The Museum of Modern Art's Department of Photography, for the handsome photographs in color and black-and-white taken especially for this book. I wish to thank all the museums, galleries and private owners who have provided photographs and information on works in their collections, and particularly Henri Marceau, Director of the Philadelphia Museum of Art and The Rodin Museum of Philadelphia, and Thomas C. Howe, Director of The California Palace of the Legion of Honor.

In the preparation of the manuscript, I have received most constructive suggestions from Professor John Galloway of Michigan State University and my colleague at Indiana University, Professor Henry H. Hope.

At The Museum of Modern Art, I have benefited particularly from the skilful editing of the text by Helen M. Franc, Editorial Associate; and I also appreciate the bibliographical assistance given by Bernard Karpel and Cornelia Corson of the Library. The last word of thanks belongs appropriately to Peter Selz, Curator of Painting and Sculpture Exhibitions. My debt to him is threefold: for his initial assignment of this book in connection with the Rodin exhibition he has so admirably directed; for his probing questions and sharing of discoveries; and finally, for his contribution of the lively postscript on "Rodin and America."

A.E.E.

CONTENTS

FOR PATRICIA MORGAN ELSEN

INTRODUCTION

IN THE LAST YEARS of his life, Rodin heard himself praised in many languages: as magician and miracle worker, magus and apostle, satanic poet and mystical philosopher, sublime genius and master sculptor. On one of his visits to England, students from the Slade School of Fine Art harnessed themselves to his carriage. When he gave a sculpture to Mexico, the art students carried it triumphantly through the streets of Mexico City. Upon his death in 1917, there was a modest private funeral at his home in Meudon; but England held an impressive memorial service, and even although this was during the First World War, Germany did likewise. Possibly no other modern artist has had such extravagant epithets and honors accorded to him and his art, nor (with the exception perhaps of Picasso) has had such international impact. The Belgian poet Rodenbach thought that, thanks to Rodin, sculpture was again a living art; others believed that he had made it possible for sculpture to be once more an effective conscience for its time. No French artist was reckoned by his contemporaries as having equaled or surpassed Rodin in giving form to the suffering, malaise and ennui of the *fin-de-siècle*. Guillaume Apollinaire esteemed him as a sublime artist whose work was characterized by purity, virility and character. Tribute came from Octave Mirbeau, who thanked him for returning sculpture to the sculptors. This reference was meant to contrast Rodin not only with those artists who habitually simply made drawings for stonecutters to transfer to marble, or commercial artists who fulfilled the demands of dealers, but also with academicians who saw sculpture exclusively as didactic, moralizing monuments to the past – a frozen literature in a rigid esthetic that had been corrupted from its origins in antiquity.

The memorable sentences of the poet, Rainer Maria Rilke, who served for a time as Rodin's secretary and remained one of his most loyal friends and admirers, stand apart with lithic durability from the glutinous sentimentality and inflated chauvinism that characterize much of the literature on the sculptor and his art. In Rilke's penetrating essay, written in 1913 (see bibl.), one finds many statements unsurpassed in the depth and lucidity of their insight. He saw Rodin as the seeker after "the grace of the great things," although "his art was not built upon a great idea, but . . . upon a craft," in which "the fundamental element was the surface . . . which was the subject matter of his art." "He was a worker whose only desire was to penetrate with all his forces into the humble and difficult significance of his tools. Therein lay a certain renunciation of Life, but in just this renunciation lay his triumph, for Life entered into his work." "He has endowed hundreds of figures that were only a little larger than his hand with the life of all passion, the blossoming of all delights and the burden of all vices,"

Rilke wrote of *The Gates of Hell.* Elsewhere, he stated: "To create an image meant to Rodin to seek eternity in a countenance . . . . Rodin's conception of art was not to beautify . . . but to separate the lasting from the transitory, to sit in judgment and to be just." And finally, "With his own development Rodin has given an impetus to all the arts in this confused age."

By the excellence of his own art, Rodin was able to persuade a previously apathetic society what sculpture could and should be. When he found it necessary to rethink sculpture down to "the hollow and the mound," he forced artists, critics and the public to take stock of their own definitions and beliefs about art. Since Rodin, this inventory and self-searching has continued and now seems limitless. When we search for the origins of modern sculpture, it is to Rodin's art that we must inevitably go. Every sculptor who came to maturity before 1914 was affected by him and had to take a stand for or against his sculpture. His was an art that could not be ignored.

What irony, then, that scarcely forty-five years after his death we should be in the midst of what is called a "Rodin revival." Measured by the centuries-long neglect of Vermeer and El Greco, the little more than two decades during which Rodin's art temporarily fell from favor seem insignificant. Indeed, talking to sculptors young and old in America and Europe today, one is surprised to hear them vow that they have *always* admired Rodin. Their statements suggest that Rodin's sculpture is so broad and varied that artists of differing temperament and taste can admire some aspect of it on their own terms.

The reasons for Rodin's fall from and return to favor are so many and complex that they could make the subject of a separate essay; some of them are indicated in Mr. Selz's postscript on "Rodin and America" (pages 191-203). Perhaps, at the turn of the century, it was natural for the younger generation to react violently against the "father" of modern sculpture, and it is no less natural for the "grandchildren" to treat him with greater tolerance and respect today. While there are still echoes of the old criticisms that his art was too literary, painterly, melodramatic, sentimental, illusionistic, or museum inspired, the charges of his infidelity to his materials are pronounced less vigorously now that we have seen the uneven results of over three decades of "truth-to-the-medium" sculpture. Nowadays the strongest resistance is to Rodin's marbles, which in most cases were never touched by his own hand. Although it is true that, by comparison with his bronzes, the marbles offer little to support Rodin's current fame, certain carved pieces have held up well and deserve thoughtful study.

It is a testimony to the soundness of Rodin's art that the present "revival" (which dates from the late 1940s) is the product of no single country, writer, critic, magazine or museum, nor is it the result of fashion. The renewed interest in Rodin is international in scope and in some respects has been more strongly motivated and abetted outside of his native France, which waited until 1962 before honoring him with an exhibition in the Louvre. The exhibitions put on in New York by the late Curt Valentin in the '40s and early '50s, on the other hand, did much to stimulate interest in Rodin's bronzes and particularly in his smaller, more improvised pieces.

Now that Rodin belongs to the past and no longer competes in the Salons and international exhibitions, it is possible to take a more detached view of his work. The myths, facts and scandals of his life have ceased to color feelings about the intrinsic merit of his sculpture. His personal and artistic shortcomings and gross lapses of taste need no longer be explained away; today they seem to make his successes even more impressive. In some ways it can be said that Rodin was a modern sculptor in spite of himself; nor does it detract from the beauty of his art to know that he entered the twentieth century almost unwittingly, and that he was dead wrong in his estimates of who would be this century's important sculptors or what their art would look like.

Rodin was the Moses of modern sculpture, leading it out of the wilderness of the nineteenth-century Salons and academic studios. Like the biblical Moses, he lived only long enough to look on the Promised Land. Not his death, however, but his steadfast adherence to naturalism and certain of its traditions prevented Rodin from entering into the new territories that were being surveyed and colonized by younger sculptors of the twentieth century.

On the occasion of the largest loan exhibition of Rodin's work ever held in the United States, it is unnecessary to champion his rescue from oblivion; but we may appropriately restore to the sculptor some of his historical context, recall his conservatism as well as his insurgency, and assess what seems most durable and significant in his art. Until the great archives of the Musée Rodin in Paris, containing correspondence, atelier notes, uncast terra cottas and plasters, and almost seven thousand unexhibited drawings, together with the materials in his studio in the Villa des Brillants at Meudon, are made fully available (presumably when, in accordance with French law, the canonical fifty years after his death will have elapsed), no complete history of Rodin's life and art can be undertaken. Countless important questions concerning dates, intentions, procedures, authenticity, influences, variants, and the mounting of individual pieces meanwhile remain unanswered. The best catalogue of Rodin's work, written for the Musée Rodin by its former curator, the late Georges Grappe, and last issued in 1944, has been out of print for over ten years and is in need of revision. The abundant examples of Rodin's art in public and private collections, however, should continue to serve as the basis for our understanding and quest. It is primarily this most precious resource that has been mined for the present study.

Bloomington, Indiana, 1963   ALBERT E. ELSEN

Young Girl with Flowers in Her Hair. 1865–70. Plaster, 20½″ high

RODIN'S CONSERVATISM

THE IMAGE of Rodin generally presented nowadays is that of the rebel. In their zeal to legitimize him as the ancestor of modern sculpture, his admirers single out certain aspects of his art for praise while conveniently overlooking others. Thus they give credence to the notion that throughout his life Rodin rebelled against the pontiffs of academic art, most of whom have since been consigned to oblivion. (Who remembers the names of Guillaume, Schoenewerk, Dalou, J.-P. Laurens and Chapuis?) This concept of Rodin as a revolutionary far in advance of his time gains acceptance by default. Today it is difficult to find even photographs to conjure up the look of the nineteenth-century Salons in which Rodin exhibited throughout his career.[1]

But if his disagreement with "the School," as he referred to the Ecole des Beaux-Arts, bears restating, so also do those large areas of agreement. Like Delacroix and Manet before him, Rodin was willing to accept official recognition and honors when they came. He was even elected to the French Academy, although ironically the official vote was cast a few days after his death. Rodin's sculpture, like the painting of Manet and the Impressionists, would have been unthinkable without academic art as a point of departure. Visualizing his sculpture in its original context, it becomes clear that in many ways his modernity is grounded in the conservatism of his time; it cannot be said to have sprung full-blown from an imagination oblivious to the style and subject matter approved by the Ecole des Beaux-Arts. Unlike Cézanne, whose art developed totally independent of official recognition, Rodin produced some of his greatest works thanks to state and municipal commissions.

His theories that art should ennoble, instruct and edify the general public, expressed in innumerable statements after 1900, allied him with his most reactionary colleagues. In his conversations on art published in 1911,[2] Rodin championed sculptors and painters who by embodying in their work the great French national virtues–heroism, wit, courage, self-denial, and respect for lofty sentiment–made the beholder feel that he himself was capable of noble deeds. "Without doubt, very fine works of art are appreciated only by a limited number; and even in galleries and public squares they are looked at only by a few. But, nevertheless, the thoughts they embody end by filtering through to the crowd."[3] Much of Rodin's own artistic education came from visiting galleries and museums and studying public monuments. His most vivid exposure to the myths of antiquity came not from books, but from works of art in the Louvre and the Salons. Looking upon the artist as a synthesizer and popularizer of culture, Rodin proclaimed that his profession should "bring within the reach of the multitude the truths discovered by the powerful intellects of the day."[4]

By the time he published these statements, Rodin himself had become the supreme pontiff of the art world. Proudly he traced the lineage of his art and dogma back not only to the Renaissance and the Gothic, but beyond these periods to ancient Greece and Rome. If this "grandfather" of modern sculpture could witness the work of his descendants and measure their ideas against his own, he would probably reconsider his belief that his mission was to provide a firm guide for the future by linking his time with the past. There is, in fact, no evidence that Rodin was ever aware of, or in sympathy with, the revolution in sculpture undertaken early in this century by Picasso, Matisse, Brancusi, Boccioni, Duchamp-Villon, Archipenko and others. The artists he admired and praised were his own satellites–Bourdelle, Despiau, Claudel and the Schnegg brothers. What he approved in the early talent of Brancusi, Maillol and Lipchitz was the evidence of their affinity with his own art or ideas concerning the imitation of nature.

A comparison of Rodin's staggering production with that of his contemporaries in the late nineteenth- and early twentieth-century Salons makes it difficult to consider him a precursor of modern art in respect to his subject matter. As was common practice at the time, a considerable portion of his *œuvre* consisted of portraits. A cursory inventory of the themes, titles and characters of his other figures reveals the extent to which his ideas and choice of subjects were common to those of other artists of the time. Characteristic themes were sin, melancholy, sorrow and despair; all stages of love, from desire and the embrace to abduction and rape; sleep, fatigue, awakening; revery, thought, and meditation. Perennial subjects were the inspiration of the artist or writer by his muse; maternity, and exchanges of affection between brothers and sisters; play and peril; self-sacrifice, death for country or for a noble cause; primeval man awakening to nature or to his own soul. Like other artists of his time, Rodin followed the old tradition of personification and used the human figure to embody time, the seasons, the elements and various flora. (In his writings and conversations, he frequently compared natural phenomena, trees, water and clouds with the human body.) His work abounded in angels, spirits and genii, nymphs, satyrs, bacchantes, sirens, centaurs, and endless bevies of dancers and bathers. Biblical figures included Satan, Adam and Eve (both before and after the Fall), Christ, St. John the Baptist and Mary Magdalen. They were rivaled by the pagan legions of Pan, Bacchus, Psyche, Orpheus, Ariadne, the Danaïd, Perseus and the Medusa, Aphrodite, Apollo and Mercury. Some of the most popular heroes and heroines derived from literature were Pygmalion and Galatea, Ugolino, Paolo and Francesca, and Romeo and Juliet. The titles in Rodin's work that refer to classical antiquity do not decrease after 1900. Rodin's titles brought him notoriety–partly because they offended public notions of how they should be portrayed in art, and partly because he could derive them from a corps of famous literary friends. His frequent practice of giving several titles to the same sculpture, or

Decorative Mask. 1878. Plaster, 55⅛" high

the same title to different works, makes identification difficult in many cases. Perhaps it was against such labels that the insurgent younger generation of the early twentieth century rebelled, believing that sculpture must be freed from literary influence and from its long subservience to illustration and mute theater.

For Rodin, to give a pair of nude figures a title from Ovid was a natural result of his education. From the time of his apprenticeship, which lasted until he was almost forty, all his decorative work in furniture, jewelry, ceramics, mantelpiece or table ornament, and architectural sculpture was identifiable with antique or Renaissance motives. On the beds, he carved appropriately tender amors: his vases were braced by bacchic idyls; balconies were supported by caryatids; fountains were flanked by huge masks of sea gods; pediments were crowned with allegorical figures representing Fame or the continents. These were the subjects that the public expected in decoration.

Rodin had a startling facility for adapting his mode to his subject, scale and medium. The gigantic and brilliant masks intended for the Trocadéro would stand out as fine mannerist sculpture and hold their own in the Bomarzo Gardens. His caryatids would seem at home if placed next to those Puget carved for the Toulon Town Hall, while his busts of garlanded adolescents belong in rococo boudoirs. He was trained both to think and work "in the manner of" *–what* or *whom* depended upon the whim of the client. In the oldest and fullest sense, Rodin trained himself long and well as a professional sculptor. Throughout his life, his talents were available for varied projects in many modes, to those who could pay for them.

p. 16

Unlike today, in Rodin's youth it was unquestioned that the young artist should work from the human figure. Unless he specialized like Barye in animal sculpture, or in floral decoration, the artist had no alternative. The study of anatomy, and drawing and modeling from the studio model, were a matter of course as part of his training. No French sculptor contested the academic dicta that the human form was the noblest means by which to express the human spirit and great ideas, and that ancient Greece and Rome provided paradigms

15

Caryatids from a Building on the Boulevard Anspach, Brussels. 1874. Stone, 61⅜″ high

for the figure's proportion, symmetry and movement. Rodin's chief dissent from the Academy lay in its failure to acknowledge or recognize the beauty of Gothic art, which he considered equaled that of antiquity. Modern appreciation of the Gothic owes a great deal to Rodin—not for his archeological information but for his meaningful reading of its form, and his ability to see it as a view of, life expressed in beautiful art that rivals the best of any period.

The nineteenth-century editions of Charles Blanc's *Grammar of the Arts of Drawing, Architecture, Sculpture, Painting* and the reviews of the Salons in the *Gazette des Beaux-Arts* enable us to reconstitute the official views of what sculpture should look like and the services it should perform. To manifest "universal life" in the grand figure style that alone could produce strong personalities represented the triumph of civilization over barbarism, for what the French thought of as their "race." These heroes were expected to show pride, majesty and grace by bodies constructed according to prescribed systems of measurement. A repertory of gestures and facial expressions existed with which to convey exalted thoughts and noble feelings. Rhetorical gestures had to seem natural in accordance with standards derived from Greek and Roman prototypes. In the characterization, eloquence and firm articulation were necessary to bring the message most directly to the beholder. Sculptors were enjoined to choose simple, uncomplicated and stable postures, leaving movement to be extended or amplified by the viewer's trained imagination. Deformity or exaggerated, strenuous movement ranked as heresy. Ugliness was not permissible in sculpture, since it would usurp that immortality of which only true beauty was worthy and would have a negative moral influence upon the susceptible. Though more widely interpreted in practice, beauty was narrowly defined by the School as selective: it was not imitative of a single model but was of a generic type, brooking no idiosyncrasies or flaws in proportion or movement. Given this fixed ideal, the sculptor's task was to find the right model. The sculptor, like his subjects, was expected to "cover his inner fire" and seem always master of himself. Correct work in marble allowed no improvisation, for this grave, formal medium was deemed the least suitable to express transient or vigorous movement. Only in sketches might the sculptor's passion be revealed, and the rough or unfinished be tolerated.

Rodin was in some respects an academician *manqué*. It was not his fault but rather his fortune that he failed three times to gain admission to the Ecole des Beaux-Arts where, in spite of his recognized technical precocity, his youthful eighteenth-century style ill suited the taste of his classically oriented examiners. Rodin admired and emulated much that the School stood for – its discipline, its master-pupil relationships, its study of the past and its provision of public monuments. Throughout his life he sought not to overthrow the School, but rather to reform and liberalize it.

His dissents from its principles and practice were nevertheless critical. One of his many statements summarizing his position on the subject was made in 1899:

> The actual fault of the School is to fear everything outside of five or six agreed-upon formulas. It has made the public likewise timid and fearful of change. Nature offers thousands and still thousands of ideas and movements, all equally beautiful. But a small number of axioms which in truth are deformities have been imposed upon us. When we see an individual or group of human beings wed to the attitudes of such academic work, we understand immediately that we are confronted with something false. [5]

Rodin would have established nature as the stern master and measure of art, with students dedicating their lives to its thoughtful imitation. On one occasion, he commented that the School was so committed to convention that it could

17

never look truth in the face. He believed that it was not theories and plaster casts but the experiences of the senses co-ordinated with the mind which brought the sculptor into contact with life, and thus with truth.

The case for Rodin's importance as an artist who rose above his own conservatism and that of his day must rest on his recognition that official art suffered from too great an esthetic and emotional distance from life, and that its content was also remote from, and irrelevant to, the deepest human needs of the time. His efforts to close these gaps gave his sculpture its distinction and produced its disquieting impact when it was first exhibited. Rodin attempted to remedy the ills of conservative sculpture and reform public art but contributed to their demise by attracting to his ideas the best youthful talent and by opening the way to more viable alternatives than he himself could ever have foreseen.

p. 20 By 1876, the date of his first major signed work, *The Age of Bronze*, Rodin was fully aware of sculpture's dilemma. He recognized that it had degenerated into a demonstration of studio rules, whose mastery produced only formal clichés and empty rhetoric. Having arrogated to itself from ancient art certain norms (often misinterpreted), the School in the name of preserving the eternal verities had shut off all possibilities for growth and flexibility. Rodin saw no opportunity under this closed system for revelation or work inspired by fresh discoveries made either from nature or from great art of the past. Temperamentally unable, in making a major, personal work, to maintain the dispassionate controlled attitude expected of the artist, he reacted against what he termed "polish versus thought" and the frigid rationalization that was supposed to dominate esthetic decisions. The most enduring of Rodin's precepts was that the artist be tenaciously truthful in translating what he *felt*. An important aspect of his modernity was that he assigned primacy to feeling as the source of art. Just as he cherished unfettered individual intuition rather than blind acceptance of rules, so he rejected the corseting of studio models in arbitrary proportions and predetermined stances that divested them of their human attributes.

Rodin's attitude toward the body was humane. None of his contemporaries had such compassionate understanding, acuity of observation, or sensitive rendering of the nude. He could find humanity in a hand or a foot. As Lipchitz has mentioned, it was the skin rather than the word that for Rodin bore the precious trace of what it meant to live at any time. His desire to make the public and artists seriously aware of sculpture, and of the possibilities for new and meaningful emotional encounters with it, was closely related to his conviction of the need for a sincere awareness of the human body itself. In the body, Rodin saw both man's fatality and his own destiny.

Much of Rodin's modernity rests upon his belief that the artist must devote his life to empirical discovery for and of himself. His empiricism, which denied the possibility of conforming to impersonal norms, was the single trait that above all others prevented Rodin from being an academician and a consistent

18

conservative. The modern ethic that the artist should work from personal experience in ways that he has individually acquired is strongly rooted in Rodin's life and art. This partially explains the natural and violent reactions against him at the turn of the century on the part of younger avant-garde artists, who consciously or not were following his ethic to its logical conclusions.

Rodin himself felt, however, that his empiricism linked him with the great artists of the past, rather than with those of the future. One of his many secretaries has nicely put the sculptor's estimate of his position: "He never claimed that he had introduced anything fresh, but that he had rediscovered what had been long lost by the academicians. The Greeks had possessed it, and so also had the Gothics. But in the official art of the day it was entirely lacking. His contribution... was therefore an act of restoration."[6] And to quote Rodin's own words: "It is not thinking with the primitive ingenuity of childhood that is most difficult, but to think with tradition, with its acquired force and with all the accumulated wealth of its thought."[7]

1. The best sources of such photographs are the albums devoted to French sculptors in the library of the Musée des Arts Décoratifs, and the Archives Photographiques of the Caisse Nationale des Monuments Historiques in the Palais Royal, Paris. Contemporary issues of the *Gazette des Beaux-Arts* contain abundant illustrations of Salon sculpture.

2. *L'Art: Entretiens réunis par Paul Gsell*, Paris, Grasset, 1911.

3. *On Art and Artists*, New York, Philosophical Library, 1957, p. 244. This is a translation, with introduction by Alfred Werner, of *L'Art*.

4. *Loc. cit.*

5. A. Alexandre, "Croquis d'après Rodin," *Figaro* (Paris), July 21, 1899.

6. A. Ludovici, *Personal Reminiscences of Auguste Rodin*, Philadelphia, Lippincott, 1926, p. 190.

7. *Les Cathédrales de France*, Paris, Colin, 1946, p. 180.

Young Mother and Child. 1865–70.
Bronze, 22⅝" high

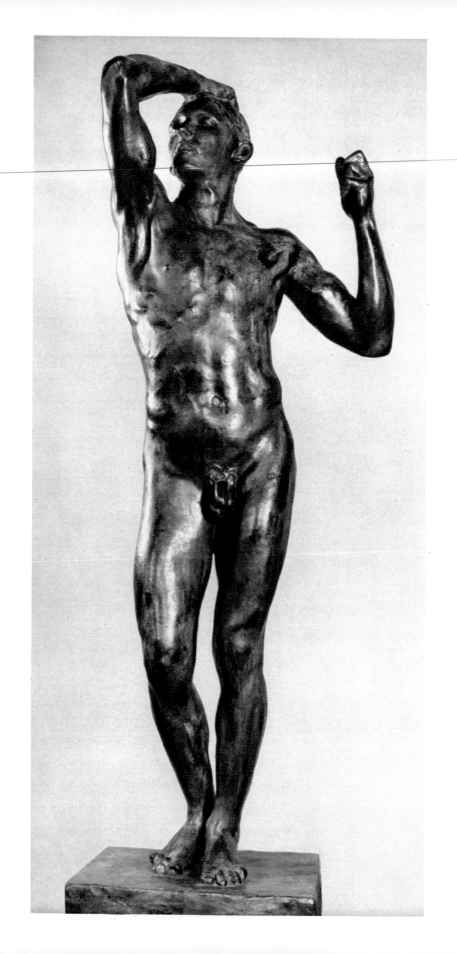

"THE AGE OF BRONZE"

N OT UNTIL he was thirty-six years old did Rodin undertake and complete his first master work, the sculpture that in his judgment marked the end of over twenty years of self-imposed apprenticeship and anonymity. (An earlier figure, *The Bacchante*, which he had worked on for three years, had been accidentally destroyed by workmen during a move to a new studio.) *The Age of Bronze* was the first full-scale figure Rodin exhibited, and it was signed with pride and satisfaction in his accomplishment. Years later he was to tell friends that he considered this sculpture rather cold and timid in modeling. He added that it and his *St. John the Baptist Preaching* "were certainly among those in which I have carried imitative art farthest."[1]

p. 29

No surface aspect of the figure's anatomy seems to have escaped his eye. Long and thorough acquaintance with the internal structure and external appearance of the body, combined with the skill in modeling he had accumulated during his long apprenticeship, resulted in a sincere and moving re-creation of the human form that seems to have evolved by biological growth. Owing largely to the physique of his chosen model, the surface offers no strong changes in value from light to dark, but a rather constant averaging of lights and half-shadows. Perhaps this was the reason that Rodin later felt the work to be cold. Even today we can understand why both in Brussels, where the sculpture was first exhibited, and in Paris there were insinuations that *The Age of Bronze* had been made from casts of the living model. In 1877 none of Rodin's critics took the time, nor were sufficiently patient and keen-sighted, to explore the work carefully and observe the subtle license he had taken with anatomy in order to enhance the truth of his sculpture.[2] Neither the public nor the critics, whose senses were numbed by the dull conventions of Salon nudity, could appreciate Rodin's vivid confrontation of a living naked body. To demonstrate the falsity of the charges against him, Rodin at his own expense had photographs and casts made of his model, the Belgian soldier Auguste Neyt, who had posed for eighteen months. Yet this evidence was never consulted by the Paris Salon jury or the critics.[3] The bitter irony of having his feat adjudged a fraud by the public deeply wounded Rodin and influenced his future in many ways.

The Age of Bronze reveals both Rodin's conservatism and his modernity. In his own lifetime, he was honored by the epithet "*statuaire.*" With this first large, uncommissioned, signed work, Rodin put himself in the tradition of the great statue makers, but he is perhaps among the last of the great sculptors for whose work the word "statue" is fitting. It is not customary today, for example, to refer to the figures of Lipchitz, Giacometti or Moore as statues, but to call them

Opposite: *The Age of Bronze.* 1876. Bronze, 71″ high

sculptures. This may be due to the long history of associations that has accrued to "statue." *The Age of Bronze* is a statue to the extent that it is a life-size standing figure, made to be exhibited, and with the artist's hope that it would be purchased by the State and placed on permanent display to edify, educate and ennoble the public. The figure with its restricted movement has a relatively stable posture and shows a handsome subject whose physical development, modeled in a lifelike manner, could inspire youth. It was provided with a base, which in turn Rodin seems occasionally to have mounted on a small pedestal. Its statuesque pedigree could be enhanced by citing as a prototype Michelangelo's *Bound Slave* in the Louvre. While today we may be liberal in assigning *The Age of Bronze* to the statue type, a French critic of 1877 called it a near miss:

> The work of M. Rodin is a study, rather than a statue, a too-servile portrait of a model without character or beauty; an astonishingly exact copy of a low type. But, if M. Rodin appears to care so little for style, he makes it all up in the living reproduction of the life of his model.... With the addition of a few modifications, such as a little more nobility in the head, a little less thinness in the lips, it may easily rise above the criticism now made against it.[4]

The critic's observations about Rodin's indifference to style and his unwillingness to choose a noble model were discerning; but there were still other aspects of *The Age of Bronze* that were to contribute to the decline of the statue type. One need never ask of the traditional statue what or who it is; its content is self-evident, either through the figure's known historical identity, the pose or some accessory. A title provided the final assurance; in fact, for many statues, the title came first, and the artist merely executed an illustration of the preconceived subject. In *The Age of Bronze,* however, there is no traditional content; there is neither literary nor historical origin; the figure's identity is not apparent; and there are no props or costume. In fact, several titles were at one time or another applied to this work: *The Vanquished, The Age of Brass, The Awakening of Humanity* and *Primeval Man.*

p. 88   With the possible exception of the *Monument to Balzac,* this sculpture received longer forethought than any single work Rodin ever undertook, and probably we can believe that when it was in the final stage he knew exactly what he wanted. But this self-confidence was not achieved easily. Over ten years later Rodin described his efforts: "I was in the deepest despair with that figure, and I worked so intensively on it, trying to get what I wanted, that there are at least four figures in it."[5] Through countless hours of meditation he seems to have striven for the right conception, the perfect pose, by which he might most advantageously display the human body and demonstrate his own gifts as modeler. Once the right pose was found, it was necessary for the model to exercise before each session to loosen his muscles and maintain exactly the same stance during months of work. From Auguste Neyt's own account, we know that the pose was neither "natural" nor drawn from life.

Seen from either side, the profile of the youth's body forms what Rodin liked to call the "console" shape, a way of posing the figure with bent knees and head jutting forward, and the chest relatively hollow, that he had discovered in Michelangelo's work during his visit to Italy six months earlier. Yet within this borrowed framework, Rodin expressed his own individuality through the close relation his modeling bore to the living subject. At a later date, he criticized Michelangelo for not having practiced the subtle modeling of the Greeks and added:

> He seems to me to have worked little from nature…. He had one figure, or type, that he reproduced everywhere and used constantly, and he took entire figures from Donatello besides using a certain movement of the wrist and foot common to the latter…. I think Michelangelo simply completed in movement and general schema, the figures whose natural principles of composition were discovered by those who went before him. [6]

Michelangelo. *The Bound Slave.* 1514–16. Marble, 90" high

But not until at least three more years after *The Age of Bronze* could Rodin himself consistently break away from the Michelangelesque pose and abandon himself completely to what was natural to his subjects.

Rodin's intent in *The Age of Bronze* is what most profoundly distinguishes it from the art of Michelangelo. He sought to show the way a single living human body looks and "to capture life by the complete expression of the profiles." [7] When working in the studio, he moved his ladder to various locations in order to be able to inspect the model from all angles and observe the interlocking profiles and correctness of the mass. He also studied clay sketches of successive views of of the young soldier by candlelight. This method of observing the profile lines, which Rodin was to follow throughout his career, was both a constant source of inspiration and a measure of his success: the meaning of his work lay not in its subject matter but in the modeling itself.

During the two- to four-hour sessions, Rodin allowed Neyt to hold a staff in his left hand, possibly to help him maintain the pose. When the figure was finished, the staff may have been changed to a spear like the one that appears in a drawing the artist made from the finished sculpture.[8] The spear together with the spirit evoked by the pose may have suggested the first title, *The Vanquished* – a natural choice in view of Rodin's long exposure to academic art. At some time before the sculpture was first exhibited at Brussels in January of 1877, however, Rodin removed the spear. Many years later he explained that he had done so because from certain angles it interfered with the view of his modeling. With the removal of the spear for esthetic reasons, there also went, in a sense, the work's iconography and subject matter. The consternation this caused can be seen in the review written by a Belgian critic, J. Rousseau: "The artist has forgotten something: it is to baptize his plaster and reveal its subject . . . . Is this a statue of a sleepwalker?"[9] Another critic complained: "Monsieur Rodin has undertaken to symbolize the hardships

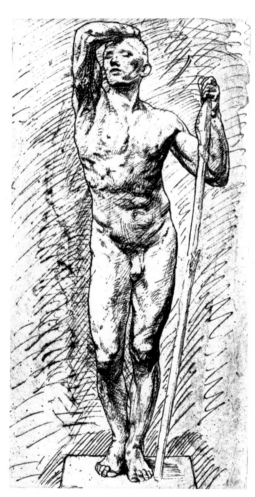

Drawing after "The Age of Bronze." 1876. Ink

24

of war; only he has neglected to give the statue an explanation or attribute that would make his intention clearer."[10] With the spear gone, interpretation had to be based partly on the gesture – itself ambivalent – but primarily on the over-all feeling that the figure conveyed. For many years this sculpture intrigued, annoyed and haunted those who studied it and led them to varied conjectures as to its meaning; for one, it was the impulse to suicide, for another, primeval man's awakening to the consciousness of life. Edvard Munch seems to have used the upper half of the body as the model for his woodcut, *The Flower of Pain* (1898); in any case, the similarity of *The Age of Bronze* to Michelangelo's *Bound Slave* would support this interpretation of anguish.

Referring to a discussion he had with Rodin in the late '80s the American, Truman H. Bartlett, commented:

> Today, in the full possession of his powers, his sole ambition is to re-live the
> time of *The Age of Brass* (*sic*), to begin again to make a simple piece of sculpture
> without reference to subject, and independent of all intricate abstraction, to
> enjoy the pleasure of the soul as its emotion is passing out of the ends of his fingers
> into a piece of clay.[11]

It is tempting to accept Rodin's avowal that *The Age of Bronze* was a "simple piece of sculpture," until one has confronted it again and again. Then the apparent simplification vanishes. The man's left arm seems to grope and project a general air of uncertainty over the whole figure. Perhaps Rodin was intuitively moving into new areas of meaning beyond his goal of accurately representing the living human body. Perhaps he was also seeking to show how the body appears when it experiences states of mind and feeling for which the cause is unknown. The indeterminate meaning of the sculpture is the natural result of the artist's search for an expressive pose, above all; and "expressive of what?" is irrelevant, or at best a secondary consideration.

Since we know of Rodin's tragic experiences during the disastrous Franco-Prussian War and his abiding concern for his country, and the disillusionment he shared with others in that war's aftermath, it is reasonable to assume that *The Vanquished* was intended to express in a general way the artist's feelings about the sufferings inflicted upon youth. We do not know if his choice of a soldier as model was intentional or merely expedient. It seems significant, however, that only two years later he completed his sketch for *The Call to Arms*. *p. 68* Rodin's persistent preoccupation with the spiritual dilemmas of his own time, as well as those of the past, may also help us to set this sculpture in its true context.

If *The Vanquished* was in fact Rodin's private response to the tragedies of war, what satisfaction the old artist must have felt when in 1907 a cast of this work – then titled *The Awakening of Humanity* – was given by a pacifist group to Léon Bourgeois, the French delegate to the Hague Peace Conference.

1. *On Art and Artists*, p. 81.

2. The following statement appeared in an unsigned article in *Etoile Belge* (Brussels), January 29, 1877: "What part casting from nature has in this plaster we need not examine here." The writer commented that he thought the figure seemed about to commit suicide. The same issue also carried a statement by Rodin which indicates that the charge of casting from life was already known to him: "If any connoisseur will do me the pleasure of investigating, I will set the model in front of him so that he can ascertain for himself how an artistic interpretation differs from a servile copy."

3. Rodin's vindication came when his unexhibited work was seen by a sculptor named Alfred Boucher. According to Rodin's onetime secretary, Frederick Lawton, Boucher visited the artist and saw him working on small-scale figures and also saw finished sculptures of a torso of *Ugolino* and a *Joshua* with upraised arms. (This last has been lost, and there seems to have been no mention of it elsewhere; perhaps it was actually the figure of *The Prodigal Son*.) Boucher induced his fellow sculptors Laplanche, Falguière, Chaplin, Thomas and Carrier-Belleuse to sign a letter to the Salon committee that had admitted *The Age of Bronze*, asking that Rodin be cleared of suspicion. (See F. Lawton, *The Life and Works of Rodin*, New York, Scribner, 1907, p. 49.)

4. Article by Tardieu in *Art* (Paris), 1877, quoted by T. H. Bartlett, "Auguste Rodin," *American Architect and Building News*, January-May, 1889, p. 99. Bartlett's long serialized article contains the best interview with Rodin ever recorded and also provides the richest source of biographical and historical material for the artist and his work of anything written in his lifetime.

5. Bartlett, *op. cit.*, p. 65.

6. *Loc. cit.*

7. H.-C.-E. Dujardin-Beaumetz, *Entretiens avec Rodin*, Paris, 1913, p. 1. It is unfortunate that this work by the then Under-Secretary for Fine Arts, which contains many interesting statements by Rodin concerning his art, is not better known. It appeared in a limited edition, was never published commercially, and has never been translated.

8. Reproduced by C. Mauclair, *Auguste Rodin*, Paris, La Renaissance du Livre, 1918.

9. *Echo du Parlement Belge* (Brussels), January, 1877. A copy of this article, which is untitled, can be found in the press-clipping file on *The Age of Bronze* in the Musée Rodin.

10. Bartlett, *op. cit.*, p. 224.

11. *Op. cit.*, p. 285.

p. 56

"ST. JOHN THE BAPTIST PREACHING"
AND
"THE WALKING MAN"

ARDENT DESIRE to dispel the previous suspicion that he had worked from casts of the live model was probably the reason that Rodin gave such a vigorous stance to his second major life-size sculpture, *St. John the Baptist Preaching*. He worked on this expansive figure in the tiny Paris studio he had rented following his return from Belgium in 1877. Biographical accounts have it that an Italian named Pignatelli, who had never served as a model, came to Rodin's studio one day, and the sculptor was so taken by his vitality and expressiveness that he stopped the visitor in the midst of a spontaneous step and ordered him to hold that pose. Rodin consistently preferred untutored models of strong character and powerful but supple build, whose naturalness permitted him to make fresh discoveries. After the finished sculpture was exhibited, the Italian was much in demand by other artists and art students, who felt that somehow the key to achieving Rodin's success lay in starting with the model he had used.

The sculptor's recent trip to Italy and his serious study of Renaissance and baroque sculpture there made at least as strong an impression as the chance visit of the model. Prototypes for the psychological intensity of Rodin's *Baptist* existed in the art of Donatello, analogous positioning of the arms occurred in Rustici's *St. John the Baptist*, and the strong movement that extended the figure into the viewer's own space could be found in sculpture by Bernini. Less relevant is the often-made comparison with archaic Greek *kouroi*. Rodin, in his own words, imparted to St. John "the progressive development of movement;"[1] he wanted the figure to be read as if it were passing through successive stages. Allowing one's eye to follow the sculpture beginning with the left leg, up through the torso, and then descending to the right leg, is equivalent to watching the figure shift its weight as if it were pushing off with the back leg as it begins the stride and were then coming down on the front foot. This explains why both feet are solidly on the ground. No such complex kinetic change can be found in archaic Greek art.

Further, Rodin knew that no cast of a stationary figure nor photograph of a moving one could give a resumé of these movements in a single pose, as he had done. His sculpture was a blow struck at the inertia of academic statuary and its frozen formulas based on earlier art. It is not the rhetoric of St. John's features and gestures that provides the real drama, but the powerful transfer of energy

Opposite: *St. John the Baptist Preaching*.
1878–80. Bronze, 78¾" high

The Walking Man (original scale). 1877–78. Bronze, 33¾″ high

Opposite: *St. John the Baptist Preaching*. 1878. Bronze, 78¾″ high

The Walking Man (enlarged scale). 1905. Bronze, 83¾″ high

Torso: Study for "The Walking Man." 1877–78.
Bronze, 20⅞" high

enacted within his body. The expressiveness of the sculpture resides in the response of the body's surface to its physical displacement as well as to the intense spiritual effort of communication. Rodin once said, "I have always endeavored to express the inner feelings by the mobility of the muscles."[2] The hard surface with its variegated modeling partly absorbs light but also violently repels it. The highly finished execution was a result of Rodin's desire to render a passionate theme with objectivity; he did not want his hand to intrude into the beholder's consciousness.

Comparison of *St. John the Baptist Preaching* with the study for it, which p. 28, 29 Rodin called *The Walking Man*, discloses the many decisions that accompanied realization of the final work. In recent years, however, it is the study that has

31

become of greater interest to modern artists and writers. Shorn of rhetorical accessories, the headless, armless body today seems both compelling and complete, surpassing the later version in its succinctness and emotional force. *The Walking Man* is not an entirely unified, consistent conception, for it combines a torso and legs that have obvious differences in the relative hardness and softness of their surfaces and the degree of their detailing. The massive legs with their heavy musculature are compactly modeled and would be impressive without the torso. The first version of *The Walking Man* was less than half life-size, and the body was erect. When it was enlarged about 1905 to over life-size, the right shoulder was bent slightly forward, injecting a touch of pathos as well as increasing the figure's driving force.[3]

p. 28

p. 30

p. 31 The original torso (existing in an imperfect bronze cast belonging to the Petit Palais in Paris) may have been inspired not only by the model, but by the fragments of classical torsos Rodin had seen and studied while in Brussels, and those in terra cotta attributed to Michelangelo that he could have seen in the Casa Buonarotti during his trip to Florence. Though Rodin's torso cannot be said to imitate any of these older examples, it comes closest to those that have been ascribed to Michelangelo.

In contrast to the highly finished body of *St. John the Baptist Preaching*, the torso sketch has been battered by ripping and cutting actions, so that its surface is more densely inflected, and there are rougher passages between the raised areas; there is also slightly less illusionistic modeling of the muscles. These raw wounds were preserved by the artist in the enlarged version, in which, although the scale is more impressive, the effect of the modeling is not as taut.

The Walking Man as finally exhibited is the antithesis of the nineteenth-century statue, for it lacks the old values of identity, assertive ego, moral message rhetorically communicated, completeness of parts and of finish, and stability. More than any other of Rodin's works, this sculpture overwhelms the viewer by the power of movement. To recent artists sympathetic to the theme of the "damaged man" in art, it may seem that Rodin intended to comment upon or celebrate the basic life force unvanquished by human suffering. There is no documentary evidence for this view. Esthetic motives rather than symbolism probably account for the battering of the figure.[4] In 1878, Rodin was passionately involved with the body as a marvelous organism instinctively able to balance itself when in motion. The sculptor, at his very best in this work, was frankly displaying tremendous insight into instinctive, rather than rational, human behavior. No sculptor before Rodin had made such a basic, simple event as walking the exclusive focus of his art and raised it to the level of high drama. The architecture of the body, the life of the flesh, the mobility of the muscles, and their poetic equivalents in clay, plaster and bronze, were the stuff of Rodin's private obsession. Man's body, its structure and its movement presented to him a more meaningful and relevant mystery than the theology of the Church, with its doctrine of God become man and His revelation to the prophesying saint. Rodin expressed his reverence for the body in the statement: "The human body is a temple that marches. Like a temple, there is a central point around which the volumes are placed and expand. It is a moving architecture."[5]

But in 1878, he was not ready to exhibit *The Walking Man* nor perhaps even himself recognize it as a completed work. For Salon taste and prudery, he converted it into a representation of the Baptist by supplying it with a head and arms, and at one time with shepherd's crook and fig leaf. It was only after he was fully established as an artist, and the public as well as visitors to his studio had become accustomed to his daring ideas, that Rodin could bring himself to exhibit *The Walking Man* as a finished sculpture.

1. *On Art and Artists*, p. 90; see also the entire chapter in this work on "Movement in Art."

2. *Ibid.*, p. 82.

3. In a recent exhibition catalogue, Cécile Goldscheider gives the date of 1900 for the enlargement (*Sculptures de Rodin*, Nice, Palais de la Méditerranée, December 1961-January 1962). Georges Grappe stated that Rodin's atelier notes provide no evidence for the date of the enlargement (*Catalogue du Musée Rodin. I. Hôtel Biron*, Paris, 1944, p. 17). The catalogue of the gigantic Rodin exhibition of 1900 simply reads: "Saint John, Baptist, A study for," with no indication given as to enlargement. According to Judith Cladel (*Rodin, sa vie glorieuse et inconnue,* Paris, Grasset, 1926, p. 133), the plaster enlargement dates from 1905, and the work was named by the men who prepared the casting. The enlarged version is definitely known to have been cast in bronze and publicly exhibited in 1907.

4. It should be pointed out that during the time *The Walking Man* was being made, Rodin made several drawings of sadistic themes inspired by Dante's *Inferno* (referred to in the next chapter); but the type of mutilation in the sculpture is dissimilar to that encountered in the drawings.

5. J. Cladel, *Rodin, The Man and His Art*, New York, Century, 1917, p. 56.

"THE GATES OF HELL"

THE GATES OF HELL is the last in a long tradition of great sculptured portals that begins with those of Santa Sabina in Rome in the fourth century A.D. Such doors as the ones at St. Michael's in Hildesheim, San Zeno in Verona, the Cathedral of Pisa, the Florentine Baptistery, and Donatello's for San Lorenzo in Florence, not only enhanced sacred buildings but made Church dogma manifest and served symbolically as the Gates of Paradise.

Rodin's portal was originally intended for a projected secular building to house the Musée des Arts Décoratifs in Paris and so lacked the religious context as well as the sacred sources of its predecessors.[1] When the proposed separate structure for this museum was not built, *The Gates* became as isolated from architecture as from theology. Although in accepting the commission Rodin realized the secular character of a building devoted to the arts of decoration, he nevertheless took his initial theme and models from medieval and Renaissance Christianity: Dante's personal comment on the spiritual condition of his age, and Ghiberti's design for the doors of the Baptistery in Florence. Yet the meaning and form of *The Gates of Hell,* which was left incomplete at Rodin's death, derive only from the sculptor's own nineteenth-century training and outlook.

Generally in embarking upon his major works Rodin had no clear conception either of their final appearance or of the demands they would make upon himself and the public. In place of this foresight was his driving self-assurance that by hard work and constant striving toward perfection he could create superior art. When the French Government's Fine Arts Committee gave him the commission for the portal in August, 1880, Rodin's statements about the project show his persistent desire to erase all public suspicion of his artistic integrity.[2] He himself chose as his subject Dante's great epic:

> They left to me the choice of subject. As much as possible I had decided to choose a subject such that the lies thrown at me could not be repeated.[3]
>
> I had no idea of interpreting Dante, tho' I was glad to accept the *Inferno* as a starting point because I wanted to do something small, in nude figures. I had been accused of using casts from nature in the execution of my work, and I had made the *St. John* to refute this, but it only partially succeeded. To prove completely that I could model from life as well as other sculptors, I determined... to make the sculpture on the door of figures smaller than life.[4]
>
> I had a great admiration for Dante. Dante is not only a visionary, but also a sculptor. His expression is lapidary in the good sense of the word. I lived a whole year with Dante... drawing the eight circles of his Hell.[5]

The surviving drawings that have been made public, from about 1875 when he first conceived the idea of working from Dante up to 1880 when he received the commission, indicate that Rodin did not methodically illustrate all the circles and their contents.[6] He repeatedly set down a limited range of themes that had impressed themselves on his memory. These involved passionate couplings of lovers, the withdrawal of a woman from a would-be lover, the abduction of women by centaurs, and the aggressive action of one male figure against either himself or another. At no later time do we find as many male figures in Rodin's drawings as in the late 1870s and early '80s. The style of these drawings inspired by Dante, compared with the one made of *The Age of Bronze* in 1876, frequently lack obvious finesse, anatomical accuracy, and the general appearance of having resulted from direct observation. In fact, they were not made from models and reveal an awkwardness of the body that is otherwise rare in Rodin's work. After these drawings, except for one made to illustrate the poem "Destruction" in Baudelaire's *Flowers of Evil*, the body is rarely clawed or torn. In the many excellent "Ugolino" studies, and in particular the drawing of a man struggling with a serpent, in which the two interchange forms,[7] Rodin used stronger shadings and textures and freer silhouettes or pen strokes than in his later style, in order to create feelings and expressions in a highly condensed, abstract way. What adds to the inherent fascination of these moody, sadistic images is that they could not possibly have been conceived as studies for the type of sculpture Rodin was making at the time. They offer an unusual and exciting view into a side of his personality that he chose largely to suppress after the early 1880s.

p. 24

Three Drawings after Dante: left, *Figure and Reptile;* center, *Ugolino;* right, *Mahomet.* 1875–80? Ink and gouache

36

One of Rodin's drawings shows how conventional were his first thoughts on *p. 39* the over-all format of the portal. From Ghiberti's "Gates of Paradise" and the Sistine ceiling came the idea of a sequence of episodes arranged in panels. The contorted nudes sketched at the outer corners are akin to those that enframe Michelangelo's Genesis illustrations. The shaded vertical patch in the upper center of the drawing may have been a notation for the setting of the figure of Eve. Densely grouped within each panel is a series of nudes, often in strenuous action but too rudimentary in outline to be identified with personages in the *Inferno*. The restrictions that the sculptor imposed upon himself by adopting this Renaissance format with its limited space and isolated events crumbled when he began to transpose his ideas and impulses into three-dimensional clay. The drawing already shows impatient notations of his desire for stronger relief and a more coloristic play of light and shade.

In the last small-scale model for the door, perhaps done late in 1880, Rodin's *p. 39* concept was developing toward a more animated and ruggedly massive form. The evolution of *The Gates* recapitulates successive stages in the history of portal art; like the later portrait of George Bernard Shaw (see pages 125-28), these phases include Gothic, Renaissance and baroque styles. Instead of fitting his sculpture to the flat surfaces of a Renaissance design, in his clay model Rodin apparently adjusted his architecture to the assertive projections of the sculpture. The heavy cornice at the top reinforces the brooding mood of *The Thinker* below. Dividing borders were ripped out or pushed back as individual groups took form, such as Paolo and Francesca at the lower left and Ugolino with one of his sons to the right. As the artist's excitement in his work awakened, he marked the whole model by gouging it with his hands; the compactness of the frame is strained with the effort of containing the explosive movements being generated within it. Rodin may have been exhilarated by recognizing both new, unlimited references in his subject and fresh possibilities for dramatic sculptural effects, freed from any literary program and unlike any he had previously achieved in his work.

Although Rodin tells us that he "lived a whole year with Dante, drawing the eight circles of his Hell," a comparison of these interpretative drawings clearly shows that they did not serve as direct sources for *The Gates*, and the artist's words tell us why:

> At the end of a year I saw that while my drawings rendered my vision of Dante, they were not close enough to reality. And I began all over again, after nature, working with my models. I abandoned my drawings from Dante. [8]

The early drawings were not completely set aside, however, for certain themes such as the embrace, or a man clutching at a resisting woman, re-emerge in the sculpture. The drawings give us a rare insight into Rodin's visionary capacity,

The Gates of Hell. 1880–1917. Bronze, 216″ high × 144″ wide × 33″ deep

Fourth Architectural Sketch for "The Gates of Hell."
1880. Pencil, ink and wash, 21″ high × 15¾″ wide

Architectural Model for "The Gates of Hell." 1880?
Terra cotta, 39½″ high × 25″ wide

which he either would not or could not translate into sculpture. His distrust of this aspect of his imagination seemingly derived from his personal criterion of "reality" in sculpture, which demanded direct sensory experience of the living model. He once commented to Dujardin-Beaumetz, "It is only in life that one searches for life. Life alone is worthy of the name of beauty, and it is not to be seen in the dream, the imagination or illusion." [9]

When he returned to the model, Rodin's inspiration accelerated, and he abandoned schemes derived from earlier illustrative or architectural sculpture. Unlike Ghiberti, Michelangelo, or any academically trained sculptor of the nineteenth century, Rodin was incapable of completely planning his entire project in advance. The strength and faults of the portal are the result of his compulsion to work through individual studies. From the time he actually began his sculpture for *The Gates*, he no longer sought guidance in older art, theology or philosophy but relied instead upon his own artistic intuition in placing and co-ordinating his figures:

> My sole idea is simply one of *color* and *effect*....[10] In the Gate I've revived the means employed by the Renaissance artists, for example, this mélange of figures, some in bas relief, others in the round, in order to obtain those beautiful blond shadows that supply all the softness. [11]

When one thinks in terms of the dark bronze casts of *The Gates*, this last statement seems puzzling, but it should be remembered that during his lifetime Rodin worked only on the plaster; the portal was not cast until between 1925 and 1928, some years after his death. He had hoped to make the individual figures in wax, attaching them to the plaster frame, which would have created even more subtle "blond shadows," but he soon found this to be impracticable.

APPEARANCE AND COMPOSITION OF "THE GATES"

More than once during his lifetime, Rodin had the figures assembled on the doors so that he could study the total impression they conveyed. They are seen today in varying sizes randomly dispersed on, against and through a graceful architectural frame. (To Truman Bartlett who saw them in 1887, the doorway appeared to be a perpendicular cross section of the world of the damned.) Although the eye may be drawn initially to the three figures surmounting the portal, and then to that of *The Thinker,* there is no firm compositional scheme, no zoned, funnel-shaped Inferno, no counterpart to Virgil to guide the eye in systematic progress from top to bottom and through the whole *Gates.* In Rodin's words: "There is no intention of classification or method of subject, no scheme of illustrations or intended moral purpose. I followed my imagination, my own sense of arrangement, movement and composition." [12]

Compositionally, the portal is a loose federation of groups, within which a formal reciprocity of movements and gestures may occasionally be found. But no sequence of figures or of actions consistently creates episodes, scenes or climactic events. There are no physical confines within which certain figures are irrevocably condemned, as in Dante's compartmented Inferno. Rodin did not want a drama of place but of persons. All is flux; only the tombs near the base of the doors suggest fixity, beginning or end. The tombs were perhaps the last major additions to the portal before Rodin's death. They draw the beholder, compelling him to stand close to the door, look up, and re-experience the first sensations of those who pass through the grave. Seen in this way, *The Gates of Hell* surrounds, absorbs and assails the eyes and feelings with the pathos of those doomed to ceaseless movement. Against the fruitless plains the dismal drama of sterile human striving unfolds.

p. 38

Rodin, who had studied the great portals of the cathedrals and no doubt also knew the tradition of the Last Judgment in painting, was surely aware that his composition had no precedent. His innovations must have been motivated by decisions based upon esthetics and significance. Exceedingly knowledgeable in the history of the interrelation between form and meaning in art, he must have recognized that in medieval and Renaissance religious compositions the stratified zones, symmetry, and hierarchical disposition of right and left, high and low, were both formal and symbolic – tangible means of expressing the order of heaven and earth. The unvoiced premise of his own work was that neither the figures nor their environment could present the stability inherent in such an orderly system.

A study of *The Gates* themselves is aided by a re-reading of the poetry of Baudelaire, upon which Rodin drew for inspiration and for the articulation of feelings that he shared with the poet. Seemingly Rodin felt that traditional compositional designs were inappropriate to show the curse of modern men, in fact of men of all ages who were afflicted with anxiety over their place and purpose in a world in which there may be no order. Man as *The Thinker* replaces Christ *p. 44* in the judgment seat; chaos supplants the legalistic hierarchies of religious and political doctrine. It was only esthetics, then, that could determine the order of the sculpture.

In saying that he sought "color and effect," Rodin meant exactly that. In his book, *Les Cathédrales de France*, and in his recorded conversations, it is apparent that he differentiated between the sculpture of Greece and that of the Middle Ages in terms of light or color. Light he assigned to the former, black to the latter; and he was able to designate the spiritual condition of entire ages by values of light and dark. In *The Gates of Hell*, he made ample provision for black through the deep recession of the lintel and leaves of the doors. Rodin relied upon light and shadow even more than on gesture and facial expression to establish the mood of his work. His disposition of groups and voids, emerging and receding shapes, was arrived at intuitively. The portal is thus seen to best advantage under strong illumination, either natural or artificial. As the light changes, so do all the interrelationships among the door's components, and not always with success. The low reliefs on the flanks which permit a fairly constant ratio between lights and shadows are the most satisfying compositionally.

The scale of the sculptures is inconsistent if one assumes that they were meant to be graded from a single point of view. In meditating upon the door, Rodin may have decided, however, that the figures should be independent of any single outside, ideal observer and that the world within the portal should instead be self-enclosed.

The Gates has balance, though not of the highest order; the flaws, such as the *tableau vivant* of the lintel, are immediately apparent. But given the enormity of the problem that the artist set himself, we may regard his failure as an heroic one.

Detail of *The Gates of Hell:* Upper part of right door panel seen from below

Although certain figures such as Paolo and Francesca and Ugolino are based p. 45 on literature, and others such as centaurs, sirens and angels on mythology or theology, one cannnot say that any traditional content exists in *The Gates*. These identifiable figures are so few in number, so scattered, so ambiguous and so intermingled with a greater number of anonymous men and women as to confound attempts to translate *The Gates of Hell* according to a literary program. Rodin may have rationalized the survival of hybrid figures in the door on the grounds that the Hell of the passions is timeless and could also encompass the creatures of fiction. ("There is no... method of subject.... I followed my imagination.") Perhaps his avoidance of specific identities for his subjects was a result of his desire to make his meaning more accessible and relevant to his own time and place – a meaning that was not in the usual province of the French painters and sculptors of his day. It is more difficult to understand the artist's statement that he intended no moral purpose. The meaning of *The Gates* is certainly moral, and as such is in fact the most moving commentary that French art of the time has to offer on humanity's spiritual dilemma.

Separated from professional, social and family life, the stabilizing co-ordinates of Church and State, the men and women of *The Gates* have been stripped bare. They have been divested of illusions, goals and hopes. Never to quit them are the passions, now their eternal, infernal punishment, for these unhappy citizens exist without law or restraint. Unlike the pathetic figures of literature and older art, the occasion of their distress is unknown. Suffering comes only from within. The body is host to relentless despair, unfocused energies and interminable fatigue. The description Rodin once gave of the spiritual significance of Michelangelo's sculpture might also apply to his own: "His sculpture expressed restless energy, the will to act without the hope of success – in fine, the martyrdom of the creature tormented by unrealizable aspirations."[13]

Although Rodin was not speaking specifically about *The Gates*, a statement that he made about the First World War in 1916 is perhaps revealing: "I am not a prophet. I only know that without religion, without art, without the love of nature, these three words are synonymous, men will die of ennui."[14] One of the strongest links between Rodin and Baudelaire, the poet *par excellence* of spleen and ennui, is their mutual recognition of the spiritual corrosion resulting from the loss of goals in their time.

Perhaps Baudelaire's strongest influence upon Rodin was not in providing vivid imagery that could be transposed into sculpture, but rather in giving the artist a precedent and an incentive to be of his time, and to reduce the historical and literary orientation evident in the first plans for *The Gates*. Although Rodin did identify some of his drawings and sculptures with *The Flowers of Evil*, it is very likely that his notations on the sketches, inscriptions on the sculptures, and

Details of *The Gates of Hell*. Above: Lower part of left door panel:
Ugolino; Paolo and Francesca. Opposite: Lintel and upper section of door panels

the titles came after the artistic fact. Rodin and Baudelaire had mutual interests and shared a concern with men as spiritually blind, solitary, restless, and incapable of embracing the suns they set up as their goals. For both, modern tragedy – unlike that of classical drama – did not involve special men or heroes whose fall from grace was due to their own unwitting acts or a conspiracy of the gods. They dealt with mankind, adrift in an empire of night; separated from, rather than being the victim of, its deity; born with a fatal duality of desire and an incapacity to fulfil it; damned on both sides of the tomb to an internal Hell of passions. The dialectic of movement and inertia set the same beat for the personages in Baudelaire's poems and Rodin's sculpture.

45

Rodin devoted much of his life to making monuments to the dead; the portal provided him with a lifelong inquest into the fate of the living. What disturbed those who saw the work in his studio was that the tragedy portrayed in *The Gates*, unlike that encountered in Salon sculpture, was within the compass of their own experience. The character of the crowd of figures is thus worthy of our attention.

These figures are too self-preoccupied to constitute what might be called an organized crowd, nor are there motives for the multitude's gathering, as there are in Dante; they do not await judgment, for example. Rodin was not consciously interpreting any particular crowd he had seen or read about, although certain groups convey a mood analogous to passages in Dante or Baudelaire. For thirty-seven years, the artist added and subtracted figures; his changing esthetic, judgment and fantasy, as well as chance encounters with interesting types, account for the over one hundred and eighty personages who populate the portal. Though the crowd is essentially the outcome of Rodin's poetic inspiration, it does not lack significance when considered from a sociological point of view. Excepting for the figures on the lintel and tympanum, what we see simultaneously is a large number of solitary individuals and couples who are not dehumanized by being in a crowd, as for the most part they act no differently because they find themselves in the company of others. Unlike a crowd situation in which individuals give up their identities and respond to the contagious feelings or actions of the majority, the personages in *The Gates* respond to their own inner dictates. Their pathos resides in their total alienation from one another. Lacking the capacity for shared emotion or mutual response, they are fated never to unite successfully with anything outside themselves. The doleful citizenry share only the common denominator of being ruled by passion— which, more than death, Rodin regarded as the great leveler of classes, professions and intellects.

Although Rodin was not a student of sociology, neither was he, as some writers would have us believe, a peasant nor a hermit immune to the culture and problems of urban life. He lived and worked in Paris, knew its best writers and artists, and responded intuitively to the plight of the individual human being. He was schooled by the street as well as by the museums. Anticipating this century, Rodin showed in *The Gates* the spiritual vacuum that could exist within those who by their professional or public achievements brought about the conception of modern material progress. *The Gates* was not, however, inspired by social or moral reform, nor did Rodin provide in it any alternatives or goals. This does not mean that he was completely pessimistic about modern man. Tragic as was his subject, Rodin derived great joy from making *The Gates of Hell*.[15] The salvation he found for himself and others – as Rilke so deeply appreciated in his letters to the sculptor – was complete devotion not to orthodox religion, but to *work*. Rodin's antidote to *The Gates of Hell* would have been his

46

abortive project, at the end of the century, for a *Monument to Labor,* in which his p. 210
intention would have been to create a speculum of those who live by manual toil.
He found salvation and its heroes in work and the worker, rather than in the
Bible and the saints.

The portal became a private monument in several ways. The decision to establish the Musée des Arts Décoratifs in a wing of the Louvre, rather than in a
building of its own, freed Rodin from having to deliver his work at a specified
time. After the turn of the century, he refunded the Government's money for
this commission. Remaining in his studio year after year, *The Gates* acquired its
own special ambiance. It was constantly seen in the light and space of the large
room located among the studios in the Government-owned Dépôt des Marbres.
Its scale was partly measurable in terms of the numerous sculptures that stood in
various states of completion before the gigantic doorway. Old photographs
make it appear as if the forms were spilling out from the door into the room it-

The Gates of Hell in plaster at the time of Rodin's death

self. The project, which the sculptor called his "Noah's Ark," became a private playground in which he indulged his fantasies about architecture and the human body. Since it was made of plaster, it was not difficult to add or withdraw figures. New ones were admitted not according to an iconographic system but to the mood they evoked, and whether they were consistent with the visual effects and general tone that the artist desired. Rodin had visions of erecting a ninety-foot-high version of the door, and his subsequent enlargement of such figures as *The Thinker* and *The Three Shades* to over life size gives some indication of what this would have entailed.

Judging by Bartlett's description, most of the work on *The Gates* seems to have been done by 1887. Thereafter, with some exceptions, much of the work was subtractive, in that Rodin would single out a figure or fragment to be re-worked or enlarged independently as a completed sculpture. From the roster of these "offspring" of the portal, we can begin to appreciate how central *The Gates of Hell* was to his art and how reflective of his many-sided personality and artistic growth.

1. For a more extensive analysis of the history and character of *The Gates of Hell*, see the author's *Rodin's Gates of Hell*, Minneapolis, University of Minnesota Press, 1960.

2. This material, not available at the time I wrote my book, changes the statement found there on page 14 concerning the lack of knowledge about the source for the portal's subject. The most meager of all the newspaper files in the Musée Rodin is that for *The Gates of Hell*; the untitled article cited in the following note constitutes its most important item.

3. Basset, article in *Matin* (Paris), March 19, 1900.

4. Bartlett, *op. cit.*, p. 223.

5. Basset, *loc. cit.*

6. The best collection of the drawings that preceded *The Gates* is to be found in the Musée Rodin. Many are reproduced in *Les Dessins d'Auguste Rodin*, Paris, Goupil, 1897.

7. Rodin refers to a passage in Dante that relates to the drawing of the man and the serpent: "You remember, too, how in Dante's *Inferno* a serpent, coiling itself about the body of one of the damned, changes into man as the man becomes reptile. The great poet describes this scene so ingeniously that in each of these two beings one follows the struggle between two natures which progressively invade and supplant each other. It is, in short, a metamorphosis of this kind that the painter or the sculptor effects in giving movements to his personages" (*On Art and Artists*, pp. 84–85).

8. Basset, *loc. cit.*

9. Dujardin-Beaumetz, *op. cit.*, p. 11.

10. Bartlett, *loc. cit.*

11. Cladel, *Rodin, The Man and His Art,* p. 28. Some years ago in an interview Mlle Cladel commented that Rodin would have been dismayed to see the door in its present bronze form because it was too dark. She came to know Rodin about 1900, when his esthetic had changed from the time of the portal's inception. I believe the younger Rodin would have foreseen the effects produced by the casts and would not have been wholly displeased with them.

12. Bartlett, *loc. cit.*

13. *On Art and Artists*, p. 210.

14. Cladel, *op. cit.*, p. 250.

15. For the artist, in Rodin's view, "All is beautiful... because he walks forever in the light of spiritual truth. Yes, the great artist, and by this I mean the poet as well as the painter and sculptor, finds even in suffering, in the death of loved ones, in the treachery of friends, something which fills him with a voluptuous though tragic admiration. At times his own heart is on the rack, yet stronger than his pain is the bitter joy which he experiences in understanding and giving expression to that pain.... When he sees beings everywhere destroying each other; when he sees all youth fading, all strength failing, all genius dying, when he is face to face with the will which decreed these tragic laws, more than ever he rejoices in his knowledge, and, seized anew by the passion for truth, he is happy" (*On Art and Artists*, pp. 66–67).

The Three Shades. 1880. Bronze, 74¼″ high on base 71″ long × 30″ deep × 7″ high.

SOME OFFSPRING OF "THE GATES OF HELL"

THE FOUR WORKS that were originally the largest sculptures associated with *The Gates* – *Adam, Eve, The Three Shades* and *The Thinker* – were direct descendants of Michelangelo's art. Rodin admired the Adam and Eve of *The Creation of Man* and *The Fall* in the Sistine ceiling because they combined the beauty of the ancient Greek nude with the medieval Christian consciousness of sin. Accepting Michelangelo's postures, with variations, Rodin chose both from his predecessor's painting and his sculpture, at times drawing from both sources in a single figure. Never did Rodin achieve that quality of *terribilità* by which Michelangelo's contemporaries were moved to such feelings of fear and reverence. None of Michelangelo's standing figures have the precarious balance of Rodin's *Adam*, which at its first public exhibition was reviled as resembling a hunchback or corkscrew. Though uncommitted to Michelangelo's canon of proportions, Rodin appears to have sought a model comparable to the Sistine Adam. His *Eve* shocked the public more than if he had thus shown the Virgin, for, as his critics pointed out, Eve was the mother of us all. To an audience conscious of the theories of evolution, it may have seemed that in *Adam* and *Eve* the artist was trying to provide the missing links. Rodin's figures impart a greater sense of self-sufficiency and inner listening than do their prototypes. Originally destined to flank the portal, they would have established the mood, as well as the source of their sinful offspring's anguished withdrawal into the self. Adam's right hand, still fixed in the life-receiving gesture, is suggestively held away from the body that turns from it in anguish; while his left arm, as Leo Steinberg has observed, is derived from that of the dead Christ in Michelangelo's *Pietà* in the Cathedral of Florence. Thus the figure is framed by the beginning and end of life; between these, his body shows its tortured existence.

Atop the door, *The Shades*, threefold variants on the figure of *Adam* minus the hands, incarnate the futility of resistance to the pull of the tomb. (In some versions of this group, enlarged and separated from the door, the hands were restored.) In *The Shades* as in the *Adam*, Rodin used another principle of Michelangelo's design – keeping the limbs close to the body, so that "you see none of those openings which, resulting from the freedom with which the arms and legs were placed, gave lightness to Greek sculpture."[1]

p. 50

p. 51

p. 51

p. 50

Above: Michelangelo. *Adam*
(detail of *The Creation of Man*).
1508–12. Fresco. Ceiling of the
Sistine Chapel, The Vatican, Rome

Right: Michelangelo. *Pietà*.
c. 1548–55. Marble, 92″ high.
Cathedral, Florence

Adam. c. 1880. Bronze, 77″ high

Eve. 1881. Bronze, 67¾″ high

Rodin's Funeral, with "The Thinker" Overlooking the Grave. Photograph taken at Meudon, 1917.

"THE THINKER"

A photograph taken at Meudon in November, 1917 on the day of Rodin's burial shows *The Thinker* gazing down into the sculptor's still-empty grave. It was the artist's own wish that this figure should serve as his headstone and epitaph. Seen in the context of the open grave and the coffin, the isolated form of *The Thinker* regains some of its morbid connotations from *The Gates*, which itself was a pessimistic speculation on the afterlife.

Rodin seems never to have indicated specifically of *what* his famous figure is thinking. Shortly before his death, discussing the sculpture with a Canadian newspaper reporter, he showed his concern with expressing *the act of thinking:*

> Nature gives me my model, life and thought; the nostrils breathe, the heart beats,
> the lungs inhale, the being thinks, and feels, has pains and joys, ambitions,
> passions and emotions. These I must express. What makes my *Thinker* think is
> that he thinks not only with his brain, with his knitted brow, his distended nostrils
> and compressed lips, but with every muscle of his arms, back and legs, with
> his clenched fist and gripping toes.[2]

52

The closest that the artist seems to have come in explaining the relation of *The Thinker* to *The Gates of Hell* was in a statement he made in 1904:

> *The Thinker* has a story. In the days long gone by, I conceived the idea of
> *The Gates of Hell*. Before the door, seated on a rock, Dante, thinking of the plan of
> his poem. Behind him, Ugolino, Francesca, Paolo, all the characters of
> *The Divine Comedy*. This project was not realized. Thin, ascetic, Dante separated
> from the whole would have been without meaning. Guided by my first inspiration
> I conceived another thinker, a naked man, seated upon a rock, his feet drawn
> under him, his fist against his teeth, he dreams. The fertile thought slowly
> elaborates itself within his brain. He is no longer dreamer, he is creator. [3]

The Thinker would thus be a personal projection of the artist, his deep thought indicative of the effort demanded by creation. Within *The Gates*, however, it should be remembered that *The Thinker* is one of those consigned to Hell. Rodin may have been suggesting that in the absence of a supreme judge such as Christ, it is the artist who must both prosecute, defend, bear witness, judge, and ironically be the prisoner of his own humanity.

The nineteenth-century precedent that epitomizes the crucial relationship of the artist to society is Gustave Courbet's allegory, *The Artist's Studio,* in which the painter showed himself as the pivot of a community separated into categories of those who do and those who do not contribute to culture. Rodin thought of society in spiritual, rather than cultural, terms and saw no divisions in the life of feelings. *The Thinker* as the artist does not mediate between groups, but it is he who must mirror the passionate side of the human condition. Beneath *The Thinker* might appropriately be inscribed: "I think, therefore, I am damned." It is through thought that men become aware of the power and consequence of the passions, which inflict self-crucifixion upon humanity.

That Rodin considered men as sharing the passions of animals is apparent in his statements, and in sculptures such as *The Centauress* in which he represents *p. 55* the tearing asunder of reason and emotion, spirit and matter. What he said in relation to *The Centauress* could apply equally to *The Thinker*:

> In themes of this kind, the thought, I believe, is easily read. They awaken the
> imagination of the spectator without any outside help. And yet, far from confining
> it in narrow limits, they give it rein to roam at will. That is, according to me,
> the role of art. The form which it creates ought to furnish a pretext for the
> unlimited development of emotion. [4]

Since its enlargement and isolation from *The Gates, The Thinker* has served *p. 54* more purposes than any other modern sculpture, confirming what Rodin's admirers considered was his ability to render a timeless, universal symbol. To cite but a few instances, this figure may be seen standing before art museums or *p. 197* philosophy departments; as an advertisement for physical culture, for electrical appliances with a built-in "brain," and for the *Syntopicon*. The countless uses, both serious and frivolous, to which this work has been put tend to obscure its

The Thinker. 1880. Bronze, 79″ high

purely sculptural character. The seated figure, deep in thought, has a rich artistic history, and certainly *The Thinker's* lineage must include Michelangelo's *Pensieroso* and *Jeremiah*, Goujon's allegorical figures on the Louvre, and Carpeaux's *Ugolino*, of which Rodin owned a cast of the preliminary study. During the nineteenth century Daumier, Delacroix and Géricault had pictured the artist clothed and seated, and inactive as a result of problems involved with creation. The formal design of the sculpture, with its compactness and divergent directions of legs and trunk, corresponds most closely with Rodin's own analysis of the manner in which Michelangelo obtained violence and constraint in a single figure. Drawings before 1880, wax and terra-cotta models show Rodin's long *p. 140* obsession with the seated figure and his grappling with such problems as the pose of the left arm, which he finally resolved by aligning it with the direction of the legs so that it contrasts with the right arm and direction of the torso. The Michelangelesque motive of the right elbow crossed over to the left thigh – a motive Rodin had noted when studying the Medici Tombs – pleased the artist by inducing an expressive torsion that conveyed the figure's mood. (After about 1882, unnatural poses of this kind were to become less frequent in Rodin's art.) The consolelike profile with its alternation of projection, recession and projection in shoulders, chest and legs came both from Michelangelo and from Gothic art, the shadows thus produced extending the dark mood. The sculpture's position high on the door led Rodin to enlarge the shoulders, lengthen the arms in

The Centauress. 1889. Marble, 28″ high × 40½″ long × 10⅝″ deep

proportion to the legs, and substitute an undefined mass for the hair, in order to allow for the spectator's lower point of view. The over-life-size version is often seen too close up, and then the topheaviness of the enlarged figure from the side view is particularly distracting.

Sentiment and popularity aside, *The Thinker* with its unnatural pose adapted from earlier art and its blatant muscular stress does not represent the sculptor's most original and successful effort. His art was to develop more personal modes of modeling and expression. The present-day use of this figure as a symbol for the abstract process of thought is perhaps as dated or unsuitable as nineteenth-century physics would be in dealing with the atom.

"THE PRODIGAL SON" AND "THE CROUCHING WOMAN"

These two inspired sculptures embody all the despairing desire of *The Gates of Hell*. They exemplify the two basic types of gestures found within the portal: the centripetal ones, addressed to the self, and the centrifugal, which grope for something that exists externally. The rhythm of *The Gates* is established by this alternate expansion and contraction, sally and withdrawal. The longing for some form of external union or communion impels the kneeling youth to seek limitless extension; he spontaneously assumes the ancient gesture of supplication, emitting, in Rodin's words, "cries lost in the heavens."[5] The woman's contracted posture (changed from that in *The Gates* by bowing the head over   *p. 58, 59* the right knee) is that of one who is denied the fulfilment of her sex and motherhood. Her silence is accompanied by the suggestion of inner listening so common among the figures of the portal. Possibly Rodin had seen a photograph or print of Michelangelo's *Crouching Youth* in Leningrad; nevertheless, *The Crouching Woman* is more expressively contorted, the limbs are locked into a greater immobility, and the pose is also one more natural to a woman. Like their brethren in Hell, these two figures unselfconsciously assume untrained gestures that are natural in moments of supreme stress; the feelings they empathically evoke in the beholder must be the measure of their validity.

Although these and similar figures express the most dire pessimism, a totally hopeless attitude toward life, it must be reiterated that they gave deep personal joy to Rodin. He was exalted by finding a meaningful posture, an exact passage of modeling like the youth's rib cage or the woman's neck:

> The sculptor must learn to reproduce the surface, which means all that vibrates on the surface, soul, love, passion, life.... Sculpture is thus the art of hollows and mounds, not of smoothness, or even polished planes.[6]

Rodin believed that he was achieving by such means what differentiated his art from that of the Greeks: "The sculpture of antiquity sought the logic of the human body. I seek its psychology."[7]

Opposite: *The Prodigal Son.* 1880–82. Bronze, 54″ high   57

The Crouching Woman. 1880–82. Terra cotta, 11¾″ high

It was not as a psychologist, however, but as a poet of form that Rodin took advantage of the poetic license of distortion that allowed him to satisfy his sense of what each sculpture required. The swelling of the youth's left hip and distension of his chest were necessary both for the balance and pace of the form and surfaces; they were exaggerations that were plausible physically, but essential sculpturally. The angle of thrust and spacing of the arms met the requirements of the bent legs and pelvis. The peculiar symmetry of the response of one part of the body to the movement of another part, such as left shoulder to right leg, was crucial for Rodin's effects of balance. The tone of each sculpture had to be sustained, as in a fine poem, not only in terms of the subject's mood but by the specific character given to the surface modeling, as for example the all-over faceting of *The Crouching Woman.*

The Crouching Woman. 1880–82. Bronze, 33″ high

In one of his greatest casts, exhibited at the Musée Rodin, the artist worked the patina himself to elicit the proper balance of browns, greens and black that would animate the surface and also sustain the tenor of the woman's emotional state. *The Crouching Woman*, characteristic of his best patina, has an unpredictable allocation of color accents, irregular in intensity and shape, which have become more brilliant rather than darker with age. Only when a fine bronze cast was made, like those that Alexis Rudier executed during the sculptor's lifetime, containing pure copper and pure malleable zinc, could Rodin rework the metal surface with tools and acids to give a rich color, further intensified by hand-polishing with soft chamois. Quite apart from the poignancy of their message, both *The Prodigal Son* and *The Crouching Woman* are esthetically beautiful, thus attaining what Rodin believed was their most enduring value as sculpture.

"I Am Beautiful" (The Abductor). 1882. Plaster, 29½" high

Fugitive Love (Fugit Amor). 1880–82? Bronze, 14⅝″ high × 19⅛″ long × 7⅝″ deep

"FUGITIVE LOVE," "I AM BEAUTIFUL,"
"THE KISS"

The sculptures entitled *Fugitive Love* and "*I Am Beautiful*" derive from *The Gates* and the works discussed above. In the first-named of these, the figure of *The Prodigal Son* has been combined with a female figure. In both works, men seek to grasp the unsubmissive forms of women, who for Rodin signified the elusive lure of the beautiful and the object of timeless passion. If we risk paraphrasing the meaning in words, we might say that within the portal (where they are found at the top of the right bas-relief) these ill-mated pairs represent humanity without moral love, or carnal pleasure sought as a substitute for spiritual fulfil-ment. On two occasions, Rodin inscribed verses from Baudelaire's *La Beauté* on the bases of his sculptures. On that of "*I Am Beautiful*" he wrote:

"Je suis belle, ô mortels, comme un rêve de pierre,
Et mon sein, où chacun s'est meurtri tour à tour,
Est fait pour inspirer au poète un amour
Eternel et muet ainsi que la matière."

("I am beautiful, oh mortals, as a dream of stone,
And my breast, whereon each dies in his turn,
Is made to inspire in the poet a love
As eternal and silent as the substance itself.")

The sculpture is a confession of Rodin's own strivings for perfection in his art, and is made all the more poignant by his inability to finish *The Gates of Hell*.

The second sculpture that bears the same inscription is a marble version of *The Kiss*. Rodin may have rejected this group from inclusion in his personal Inferno, feeling that the subject lacked the tragic involvement that the portal required, or that its form was too self-enclosed to unite with adjacent figures. In many ways the original small bronze version of *The Kiss* is esthetically superior to the over-life-size marble version, from which all the vibrancy of Rodin's own hand has been lost by the stonecutter. In the half-life-size bronze, the surfaces are more eventful, the man's right hand more sensitively modeled, and its finger tips more tensely related to the flesh of the woman's leg. (Some fingers touch, others hold back–in miniature, the theme of the entire work.) The quality of restraint and desire, of giving and withholding, is more sharply felt in the bronze.

The male figure of "*I Am Beautiful*" was one of Rodin's favorite forms. Seen from the front, the chest area has strong affinities with antique torsos like those he had seen in Brussels and which he was later to acquire for his own collection. The back shows that forceful, expressive modeling that the artist accentuated in *The Gates*, so that in spite of its position high up in the right bas-relief, it can be clearly seen in the figure clinging to the base of the lintel to the lower left of *The Thinker*; it occurs again in the group (known as *Avarice and Lust*) next to the tomb at the lower right, where the man, inverted, clutches the body of a woman. This back may have been inspired by, or in turn inspired, those of *The Burghers of Calais*, for its exact date is not known. Rodin habitually orchestrated a given figure that pleased him by placing it throughout the doors in ways that varied its context, axis, angle of sight and meaning. In the version of this figure that clings to the lintel, he blinded the eyes, thereby deepening the man's affinity to Baudelaire's Icarus, who was broken by the love of beauty and to whose sightless vision came only memories of suns.

The poem to which Rodin was most continuously responsive, however, was neither *The Flowers of Evil* nor *The Divine Comedy*, but that of human flesh. The record of life from infancy to senility, unwritten or harshly inscribed, found its way into *The Gates*. In the left bas-relief, the sculptured surface modulates as it encompasses a child, a young woman and a pathetic crone. The inspiration for

p. 44

p. 34

p. 84, 85

62

the last of these, and for a related sculpture, did not come from François Villon's poem "She Who Was Once the Helmet-Maker's Beautiful Wife" ("*Les Regrets de la Belle Heaulmière*" from *Le Grand Testament*) but from an aged Italian, formerly a professional model, who had posed for one of Rodin's assistants, Jules Desbois. Having seen Desbois' sculpture (now in the Musée Rodin), Rodin obtained the old woman's name and had her pose for him in a more moving and imaginative way, confronting with mingled despair, resignation and defiance the evidence life had inscribed on her body. Presumably after having done the p. 64, 65 free-standing sculpture, about 1885, he combined this figure with the girl and

The Kiss. 1880–82? Bronze, 33⅝" high

"*She Who Was Once the Helmet-Maker's Beautiful Wife*" (*The Old Courtesan*). 1885.
Bronze, 19⅞" high

"*The Helmet-Maker's Wife*," rear view

child to form the tragic trilogy in the portal relief. More relevant than Villon's poem is the sculptor's own idea about ugliness in art:

> When an artist... softens the grimace of pain, the shapelessness of age, the hideous-ness of perversion, when he arranges nature – veiling, disguising, tempering it to please the ignorant public – then he is creating ugliness because he fears the truth.[8]

If one were to select a sculpture that more than any other epitomizes the meaning of *The Gates*, the choice could well be that of a single head – the *Head* *p. 56* *of Sorrow*. Although Rodin had used this head for such male figures as *The Prodigal* *p. 45* *Son* and for Paolo in the version of Paolo and Francesca in *The Gates,* later in 1905 he remodeled it into a likeness of Eleonora Duse. The bisexual nature of the head makes it all the more appropriate. Edvard Munch may have seen it on one of his visits to Paris, for like the subject of his famous lithograph, Rodin's *Head of Sorrow* is a romantic *Cry of the World* – the issue of all human anguish.

1. *On Art and Artists*, p. 208.

2. This article appeared in the periodical *Saturday Night* (Toronto), December 1, 1917.

3. Letter written to the critic Marcel Adam and published in an article in *Gil Blas* (Paris), July 7, 1904.

4. *On Art and Artists*, p. 175.

5. V. Frisch and J. T. Shipley, *Auguste Rodin,* New York, Stokes, 1939, p. 424.

6. *Ibid.,* p. 203.

7. *Ibid.,* p. 246.

8. *On Art and Artists*, p. 64.

Head of Sorrow. By 1882 (remodeled 1905 ?).
Bronze, 9¼″ high

The Burghers of Calais (detail). 1884–86. Bronze.

RODIN AS A
MONUMENT MAKER

"THE CALL TO ARMS"

Throughout his career, Rodin often sought to make public monuments. Paradoxically, he contributed to the fall of the statue and of the monument, while opening up new possibilities for expressiveness at the expense of subject matter. When he tried to make the monument more relevant to life, more humane through its form and meaning, he produced an art that laid bare what was deemed too private for such exposure. Rodin introduces the dilemma of the modern sculptor who would like to work for an architect or for a public commission, but whose art is of so personal a nature as to be inimical to the traditional views of such patrons.

Between 1878 and 1882 Rodin tried unsuccessfully to obtain five commissions. His most notable lack of success was his 1878 project for a monument to commemorate the Franco-Prussian War of 1870. Not only was his terra-cotta sketch rejected by the committee, it was not even ranked among those receiving honorable mention. Rodin's ambitions for this project were not realized until after his death, when in 1920 an enlarged version of *The Call to Arms,* in bronze, was paid for by the Dutch Government and set up as a war memorial to Verdun.

The Call to Arms is the vigorous offspring of François Rude's *La Marseillaise,* *p. 68, p. 69* the finest embodiment of the grand style in nineteenth-century sculpture and a work deeply respected by Rodin. Besides demonstrating his acceptance of Rude's symbolic personification of war and the national spirit, *The Call to Arms* and later *The Burghers of Calais* help us to evaluate Rodin's individuality as a *p. 71* public image maker. Rude's over-life-size relief on the Arc de Triomphe combines heroic theme and style. Civilization's supreme moment comes as a call to arms, to which men of all ages (six are made to seem an army) unhesitatingly respond. These are heroes who act, and who with one stride impart a sense of irresistible momentum. Rude's clarity of exposition and dramatic phrasing are impeccable, for, as in a beautifully designed machine, all parts assume their rightful place and work in concert with cumulative effect. In a fine interpretation of this sculpture, Rodin defined the successive stages of the drama's evolution.[1] (It was thus that he desired his own monuments to be read.) In Rude's orchestration of major and minor movements, the rectangular composition is

Study for "The Call to Arms" (La Défense). 1878. Bronze, 45" high

dominated by a concerted sweep from lower right to upper left, culminating in the sword blade that seems an extension of the body's thrust. The energy that is transformed from potential to actual within *La Marseillaise* is purposeful and always in focus; each figure's placement is made to appear inevitable. The military paraphernalia of weapons and uniforms never obtrude against the more important, firmly muscled bodies. As a sub-theme, *La Marseillaise* calls for a Spartan physical culture at the service of a single-minded national purpose.

Rodin's *Call to Arms* shares the stirring masculine qualities of *La Marseillaise*, but with pathetic overtones. The warrior is wounded and must be rallied from death by a spirit whose bent wing fails to impart the invincibility of Rude's climactic figure. Early in Rodin's work, we see that his heroes are people to whom violence has been done, and who are vulnerable in flesh and spirit. This frank acceptance of human weakness probably dismayed the committee that negatively judged and then ignored Rodin's entry. The expressively contorted configuration of the warrior, recalling Michelangelo's dead Christ in the *Pietà* p. 50 in the Cathedral of Florence, prevents the beholder from sensing that clarity

François Rude. *La Marseillaise*. 1833–36. Stone, over life-size.
Arc de Triomphe, Paris

of purpose and symbolic direction found in Rude's relief. Rodin's allegorical figure of France convulsively discharging her appeal in all directions would likewise have compared unfavorably with its earlier militant counterpart. Rude preserved the toughness of stone in the bodies of his volunteers, augmenting the masculinity of his conception; Rodin's warrior is so roughly modeled as to present infirm surfaces, and their flux increases the instability of the precariously posed body.

Conservative critics would have been still further dismayed by the agitated irregularities of the silhouettes in *The Call to Arms*, which strongly divert the viewer's eye from sustained focus on the inner masses. Far more baroque than classical, Rodin's composition aggressively lunges and bulges into its surrounding space, without the remoteness and graceful turning back of the edges that Rude had achieved in his relief. Compared to Rude's group, the postures of Rodin's two figures are too restless and interdependent for stability and violate the classical preference for a durable pose. The vehemence of Rodin's work scarcely suggests that its creator had "covered his inner fire." More revealingly *p. 20, p. 29* than his earlier *Age of Bronze* and *St. John the Baptist Preaching*, this precious sketch tells us that by 1878 Rodin had recognized his own passionate forces and sought to use his gifts to overcome the inertia which official sculpture justified in the name of classical rectitude. As is so often the case, in the later enlarged version of *The Call to Arms* the concentrated vigor and power of the initial small sketch has been diluted.

"THE BURGHERS OF CALAIS"

The first major public commission for which Rodin successfully competed was a commemorative monument proposed by the city of Calais in 1884. When he began work on what was to become known as *The Burghers of Calais*, Rodin was undertaking one of the last great works of public sculpture inspired by a specific historic event. He was to re-create from the late-medieval *Chronicles* of Froissart the heroic sacrifice of the six leading citizens of Calais who, in 1347, during the Hundred Years' War, had donned sackcloth and rope halters to give themselves to King Edward III of England as hostages in return for a lifting of the bloody eleven-months' siege of their city. The sculpture was to be illustrative in the most honorable traditions of art. Rodin was to bring the event to life through his readings and visits to the site, but above all through finding the right human, rather than artistic, models.

The commission had many exciting elements for Rodin. He believed, like Delacroix, that art could rival literature as well as be inspired by it, and that the subject should be important and well known. Here he had a great story of moral sacrifice vividly told – one which provided him with latitude for his own imagination. The episode had taken place in medieval France, the period that

The Burghers of Calais. 1886–87. Bronze, 85″ high including base 91¼″ long × 70⅜″ deep × 6½″ high

the artist loved the best and knew the most profoundly. This was to be an occasion for him to treat a theme both medieval and timeless, in a style that he deeply believed was compatible with Gothic art, yet right for his own day. Finally, his work would be exhibited in an important public place and would contribute to a sense of identity between the community of the living and the dead. Encountered daily, it could serve as a modern equivalent of the religious art of the past, which by joining art and life had inspired reverence and exalted feelings. Small wonder that in the flush of his initial enthusiasm, Rodin persuaded the committee to accept six figures for the price of the anticipated one!

Quick to die was the committee's hope that Rodin would make a single stoic figure of the oldest Burgher, Eustache de St. Pierre, perhaps flanked in a pyramidal composition by allegorical figures of Fame and the city. This would have been the predictable design of a fashionable sculptor like Barrias, who followed such a scheme in his monument to Victor Hugo. The patrons' conviction that, alternatively, Rodin should show all the hostages meeting their death proudly, rather than struggling with the infirmities of body and spirit, was never completely overcome throughout years of argument and even up to the final installation of the work in 1895. Possibly in retaliation, the committee refused to grant Rodin the site he desired – the square before the medieval Town Hall; *The Burghers* was first placed in front of a public garden and was not moved to the square until 1926. For over ten years, Rodin's energies, time and thoughts were diverted from total concentration on his sculpture by threats of shortages of funds, criticism of sketches by the press and the public, and haggling over casting costs and the character of the base for the figures.[2] Besides meeting many of the preliminary expenses for models, casts and armatures out of his own pocket, Rodin realized no profit when the work was finished, and he saw his plans for the base as well as for the site compromised. In a sense, *The Burghers of Calais* is a personal monument to its creator's perseverance and his ability to keep the true worth of his art always in mind.

The Burghers before the Calais Town Hall

First Maquette, "The Burghers of Calais" (detail). 1884. Plaster, 13⅜" high × 13½" long × 9½" deep

THE CONCEPTION AND STUDIES FOR "THE BURGHERS" Character-
istically, Rodin was quick to find his initial conception for a commission and
agonizingly slow to complete it. In November, 1884, he presented to the Calais
group a small clay sketch, about which he wrote to Mayor Dewavrin, a constant
friend and protector during the trying decade:

> The idea seems to me to be completely original from the point of view of archi-
> tecture and sculpture. The subject imposes an heroic conception and the
> ensemble of these six self-sacrificing figures has a communicative expression and
> emotion. The pedestal is triumphal and has the rudiments of a triumphal arch, in
> order to carry, not a quadriga, but human patriotism, abnegation and virtue....
> Rarely have I succeeded in giving a sketch such élan and sobriety.... Eustache de
> St. Pierre, alone, his arm slightly raised, by the dignity of his determined movement
> leads his relatives and friends. [3]

What Rodin felt to be original was his cubical composition that harmonized
with the shape of the base. In still another letter the design was defended: "The
cube gives expression. The cone is the hobby-horse *[dada]* of the students who
vie for the Prix de Rome."[4] The device of envisaging his figures within some

imaginary geometrical volume to measure its movement and insure balance was one that Rodin had been taught at the Petite Ecole when studying with Lecoq de Boisbaudran, and it was used by academic artists as well. Rodin once explained that in constructing a single figure: "Everything is built in the finest equilibrium; and everything, too, is enclosed in a triangle or a cube, or in some modification of them."[5] Feeling, however, that triangular compositions of more than one figure were cold and inhibited movement, he chose for *The Burghers* a roughly straight line of heads that

Anonymous French Master. *Head of Christ as Man of Sorrows.* 16th century. Painted stone, 11¾" high

provided maximum freedom, while still preserving architectural coherence.

p. 73 The sketch for the ensemble shows a tightly packed group, heavily encumbered by drapery and ropes, all advancing except the faltering figure at the extreme right, who like his counterpart in the final sculpture grasps his head in his hands. When Rodin wrote that the quadriga had been replaced, he was referring to academic monuments, atop whose lofty pedestals soared chariots p. 38 drawn by four horses, driven by pagan gods. Just as in *The Gates of Hell*, on which he was working during the same years, Christ as Judge had been supplanted by man, so in *The Burghers* Rodin struck a blow against the traditional monument by making humanity depose the old pagan gods and academic allegorical figures. The elaborate pedestal, for which he once planned bas-reliefs, was part of the commission; while he was shortly to reject its triumphal mode, Rodin seems at time to have vacillated between a high and a low base. When he finally decided to remove an artificial base, he quite literally, rather than figuratively, took humanity off its pedestal – a further violation of the monument tradition.

The artist was specific on the moment in Froissart's *Chronicles* he had chosen to commemorate in his composition:

> Originally I thought of the Burghers leaving the market place. In the confusion of the goodbyes, only St. Pierre has begun to walk in order to cut short the painful scene....[6] He leaves the city and descends toward the camp; it is he who gives the group the aspect of a march, of movement. Eustache is the first who descends, and for my lines, it is necessary that he be thus....[7] They are tied voluntarily by the same sacrifice, but each one responds individually according to his age and situation. These people live through their legendary expressions, and their grouping must be found through their silhouettes in the atmosphere, and of necessity against the background of the sky made possible by a low pedestal.[8]

74

Froissart recounts that the hostages, led by their army captain, had to pass through two gates, those of the city and those of the defensive barriers: "The gate was opened and he issued out with the six Burghers, and closed the gate again." By coincidence, Rodin was simultaneously at work on *The Gates of Hell*, which has as its theme those who have passed through the gates of life. Above the sculptured doorway stand three contorted figures who, like the Burghers, personify the futility of resistance to death. Their gestures, unlike those of the Burghers, are still derived from earlier art, having prototypes in the sculpture of Michelangelo; those of the Burghers, however, were discovered in actual life and constitute an important step in Rodin's development of a personal art. As a result of two major but unrelated commissions, the sculptor had an opportunity to express his most private reflections on the meaning of mortality. He came to realize that these thoughts, as well as their embodiment in his art, must originate within himself and could not be acquired from tradition. By becoming intimately involved in these tragic themes, Rodin believed he could achieve an honesty and naturalness of expression that would readily communicate with the public. In actuality, he only alienated much of his audience, conditioned by the artificial drama of Salon sculpture.

Heroic Head: Pierre de Wiessant. By 1889. Bronze, 32¼" high

Studies for "The Burghers of Calais."
1884–85. Plaster, each c. 27½″ high.

Above: left, *Jean de Fiennes;*
center, *Jacques de Wiessant;*
right, *Eustache de St. Pierre.*

Below: left, *Jean d'Aire;*
right, *A Burgher.*

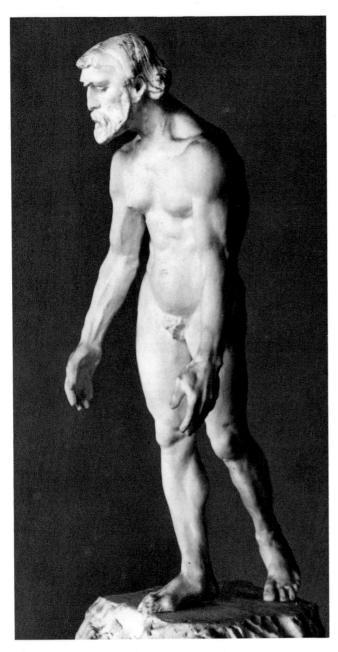

Nude Study for Eustache de St. Pierre. 1884–85.
Terra cotta, 12¼" high

It is fruitless to search for medieval counterparts from which Rodin may have taken direct inspiration for *The Burghers*. The hostages' *Via Crucis* first brings to mind the carved stone narratives of late Gothic Breton Calvaries, but the comparison does not survive a juxtaposition. Rodin himself mentioned medieval analogies for his work only with respect to his desire that it should be accessible and placed on a low pedestal: "to allow the public to penetrate to the heart of the subject, as in the Entombments in churches, where the group is almost on the ground."[9] As a result of his many trips to Gothic monuments throughout France, he was undoubtedly familiar with the sculptured *Pietàs* of the Middle Ages, as well as with the famous *Entombment* at Solesmes. More reminiscent of late Gothic inspiration for details such as the head of Pierre de Wiessant are sculptures of that period in the Louvre showing Christ as the Man of Sorrows. As Rodin recognized, the spiritual anguish expressed in this type of sculpture was unknown in ancient Greek art. But while medieval society reserved the holiness of suffering for images of Christ and the saints, Rodin's humanistic spirit urged him to impart to the living and to his contemporaries attributes previously conferred by the halo. In this regard Rodin is related to an important aspect of late nineteenth-century art exemplified by Vincent van Gogh and Edvard Munch.

p. 75
p. 74

During the first years of the project, Rodin devoted considerable time to developing the characters of the individual Burghers. The *Chronicles* provided little information beyond names, ages and status to aid the sculptor in his search for appropriate models. These included for a time the painter Cazin, possibly Legros, and Rodin's own son, Auguste Beuret, who posed at least for the Burgher who carries the citadel key, in the rear of the final group. The heroic types of Rude's relief could not satisfy Rodin. To bring these medieval heroes to life meant that their human drama had to be enacted through the flesh-and-bone frames of living men. (This concept resulted in the "beefsteak art" against which Maillol and Brancusi later inveighed.) Rodin sought and found models whose beauty lay in their strength of character, not in their appearance. Donatello's Prophets on the Campanile of the Florentine Cathedral, which he had seen a few years before, may have served as precedents; for Rodin, however, the model had to be seen and portrayed in movement in order to embody the character he sought. He chose models whose moving, naked bodies suggested a maturity hardened by arduous physical labor or combat rather than by gymnastic exercise. In the first small clay sketches, this desired rugged toughness comes through, in spite of the prominent sackcloth and ropes. None of the striding figures in these sketches possesses the traditional equilibrium that had given visual stability to Rude's soldiers. More daring than Rodin's *Walking Man* and *St. John the Baptist Preaching* of a few years before is the forward tilt of the hostages' bodies, seemingly weighted down by the dual pulls of harness and of

p. 76

p. 28
p. 29

Opposite: *Torso: Study for the Burgher Pierre de Wiessant.*
1885–86? Bronze, $74\frac{7}{8}$" high

78

duty. Where an equal distribution of weight between the two striding legs had given the figure of the Baptist a proud and upright air, a shifting of the balance to the front foot coupled with the bowed heads, necks and shoulders of the Burghers produced the new pathos Rodin desired.

p. 76   In spite of the roughness of their features, the first figure sketches on a small scale are often mordantly characterized; one of the older figures, for example, seems almost skeletal in his birdlike profile. When the sculptor was satisfied that his small sketches were true to his intent, he had his assistants enlarge them by the pointing method, at first to half-life-size, until he was ready for the final six-foot scale that he had decided upon by 1885.[10] Like David and his academic *p. 77* followers, Rodin insisted upon first completing his figures in the nude before draping them, so that he could be assured of the modeling and rightness of the body before it entered into its dialogue with the drapery. The care with which

The Mighty Hand (Grande Main Crispée). 1884–86.
Bronze, 18¼″ high

Composition of Heads and Hands from "The Burghers of Calais."
Plaster, 8¼″ high × 11″ long × 9¼″ deep

he created the surface of the entire bodies, even though they were later to be partially concealed, is suggested in Edmond de Goncourt's brief journal entry of April 17, 1888: "Rodin turned on their stands the life-size clay forms of the six hostages of Calais; modeled with a powerfully charged realism, and having the beautiful holes in the human flesh that Barye put in the flanks of his animals." From his youthful study with Barye at the Jardin des Plantes, Rodin had in fact learned to construct human and animal bodies from the skeleton; but Barye's art was even more important to Rodin than his instruction, and Edmond de Goncourt's observation of the flesh treatment was astute.

A partial figure, life size, of one of the Burghers, showing a swaying torso, *p. 79* remains as a reminder of Rodin's method of working by addition and subtraction. Heads and hands were at times conceived separately and tried on different torsos until the appropriate combination had been achieved. This procedure differed from that of the academicians, with their fixed types for bodies and faces that could never be interchanged lest the whole figure's generic character be disrupted. Rodin, however, dealt with particular models, specific bodies, hands and faces; and his gift was the ability to synthesize a figure so convincingly that the entire body seemed a unique biographical statement. Some parts intended for *The Burghers* never found permanent attachment, such as *The Mighty Hand* which today exists in isolation. But this expressive hand, along with truncated torsos and heads, somehow epitomizes the anguish of the group

81

as a whole. Rodin was so preoccupied with the project and its parts that he

p. 81 assembled several heads and hands in a relief surmounted by a winged figure (one of the damned from *The Gates of Hell* transformed into a Victory). The sentimental exchange of embraces and shared grief in this small model is totally unlike the final large-scale group.

It is hard to judge whether Rodin had from the beginning a set composition for his figures, nor is it possible to assess how much he changed the life-size Burghers once they were put together. Since the figures were on stands that allowed them to be revolved, he undoubtedly indulged in countless hours of recombining their forms. Shortly before 1912, Rodin confided to a friend that one of his original plans had been:

> To fix my statues one behind the other on the stones of the Place, before the Town Hall of Calais, like a living chaplet of suffering and of sacrifice. My figures would so have appeared to direct their steps from the municipal building toward the camp of Edward III, and the people of Calais of today, almost elbowing them, would have felt more deeply the tradition of solidarity which unites them to these heroes. It would have been, I believe, intensely impressive. But my proposal was rejected. [11]

p. 71 THE MONUMENT Rodin's talent for composition was not great, and admittedly there are certain views from which the arrangement of *The Burghers* seems more successful than others. He himself recognized this and regarded six or seven prospects as the most satisfactory. In the statement quoted above (page 74), the artist indicated that the union of the Burghers was to be an esthetic one, achieved by the right relationship among their silhouettes. The absence of psychological interaction that might unite the figures through glance and gesture may be explained by Rodin's desire to indicate that in his last moments each hostage must come to terms with himself. Detesting the struck pose and superficial rhetoric of academic art, he once commented: "In Paris I am the antagonist of the theatrical art of the School." [12] The unselfconscious gestures of *The Burghers* have been wrung from true states of feeling. Compared to those of Salon art, they seem natural, because Rodin drew from what was instinctive in his models. His sincerity saves his work from melodrama; and if today these gestures seem extravagant, it is perhaps because Rodin with a poet's sense and sculptor's eye enlarged and exaggerated the movements so that their clarity and ready visibility might insure impact on the beholder.

p. 84, 85 The grouping of *The Burghers* is a type of *ronde*, as if one figure were seen in successive moods and moments. (The possible origin and morbid connotations of the *ronde* theme are discussed on pages 155-56.) To re-experience Rodin's concept, it is necessary to focus successively on the natural pairs and triads formed by the figures and to find the rhythmic sequences set up through the ankles, calves, drapery, backs, shoulders, hands and heads. "I have thought at length on this composition to the extent that I spent five months in studying it." [13] Rodin

82

wanted the people of Calais to "read" the heroism in his figures; but being above all a sculptor who loved modeling more than history, and having a more acute sensibility to the body than to the word, he also wanted the sympathetic viewer to savor what was poetic in his form.

To take in the entirety of *The Burghers of Calais* from any single point of view makes unremittingly exhausting demands upon one's senses and feelings. More than in any other work of Rodin's, the surfaces of *The Burghers* demand to be *felt* as well as seen. (Rodin wanted children to play on the sculptures and the patina of the bronze to result from daily handling by the passersby. How different an education for the public from that envisaged by other monument makers of the time, or by the Calais committee!)

With one's eyes closed and the mind totally receptive to the sense of touch, one can comprehend how fully life has been transfused into the bronze. Rodin complained that it would take him a year to describe one of his sculptures completely. The effort to verbalize the response of the fingers as they move over a single exposed forearm of one of the Burghers is a reminder of our impoverished vocabulary, restricted visual literacy and limited first-hand knowledge of the intimate construction of our own bodies. Within an area confined to a few inches on the sculpture, each fingertip will encounter surface inflections of a different character; feeling one's own arm, one gains the impression that the surfaces conceived by Rodin are more richly complex. Only when one inserts the hand into the furrowed backs or deep-socketed eyes of the sculpture can the mind be convinced of what the eye has seen.

When the figures are seen at ground level, it is possible to look between them and experience the decided intervals between the bodies–spacings reciprocally involved with their positions and with the fall of their drapery. *The Burghers* gave the sculptor a unique occasion for lovingly imparting to his work a lifetime of serious drapery study. Although he knew the use of drapery by Donatello, Claus Sluter and Claus de Werve, Rodin needed no prototype for his intuitive grasp of the unclassical, medieval principle of employing the draped garment as an expressive extension of its wearer's state of mind. The sheer weight and precipitous fall of the folds in *The Burghers'* sackcloth confirm the fatal pull of the grave against which the figures resist. Studied by itself, the drapery reveals an alternation of projections and almost brutal incursions into shadow, along with subtle deviations from the perpendicular. Rodin proves himself to be a sculptor highly sensitive to the diagonal. Seen under strong sunlight, the drapery creates an epic of black like that which Rodin passionately admired in Gothic art, and which makes his style the antithesis of Impressionism. His poetic sensibility to shadows was never expressed more beautifully than in his statement: "To model shadows is to create thoughts."[14]

The citizens of Calais were not fully prepared for this sculpture, which by revealing the private agonies of their hallowed Burghers denied the cherished

The Burghers of Calais. 1884–86. Bronze, 85″ high including base 91¼″ long × 70⅜″ deep × 6½″ high

Alberto Giacometti. *City Square*. 1948. Bronze, 8¼″ high (base 25⅜″ long × 17¼″ deep)

ethos of official art.[15] A letter of 1885 to Rodin from the committee included the complaint: "We did not visualize our glorious fellow citizens proceeding to the King of England's camp in this way; their dejected attitudes offend our religion." Rodin demanded an identification which was at once too great and too unfamiliar; it was a shock to see a centuries-old legend share the pulse and heartache of the living. The artist had made the public monument too private, too relevant, too vivid an education for the young, who were supposed to be schooled in textbook virtue. "They would have preferred gestures *à la Marseillaise*, whereas I intended to show my citizens sacrificing themselves as people did in those days, without publishing their names."[16]

When we compare *The Burghers of Calais* with a more recent sculpture, Giacometti's *City Square*, we can begin to understand the gain and loss in modern sculpture since Rodin. In replacing the gods on the pedestal by men, and then by removing the pedestal itself, Rodin took a vital first step. Giacometti then turns men into anonymous figures walking on a street that has become part of the environmental context of his sculpture; they share a space that the artist has created. Rodin's Burghers move within our own space, and their context is that of the actual square in Calais. The space in *City Square* is greater than the figures, but it belongs only to them and is not shared by us, the spectators. Both artists have shown men in isolation, but the psychological, emotional and spiritual causes for this state, which were important considerations for Rodin and which give his figures their pathos, have been rejected by Giacometti. For him, the solitary man is a fact of existence; although minuscule in the cosmos, he is not to be pitied.

p. 72

As an object of mystery and endless contemplation, the human body is

86

supreme to both artists—which only adds to the elusiveness of its perfect rendition. For Rodin, the body he contemplates has to be within the reach of his fingers; for Giacometti, always across an interval that prohibits touch. Movement is translated by Rodin in terms of physiological life – the marvelous complex of skeletal and muscular interaction and gravitational response as the body passes through successive kinetic states. In a more detached way, Giacometti shows us the depersonalized body in movement, as a remotely observed visual phenomenon, so drastically reduced by effects of light and vision as to border on dissolution. While both artists rely upon silhouettes seen against space, the intervals between the figures are more important and complex in Giacometti's work. Ironically, in this comparison, Rodin's sentimental associations with heroism are probably more embarrassing to the modern eye than Giacometti's startling isolation of a pedestrian subject, because the latter is closer to our daily experience.

Jean de Fiennes (detail of *The Burghers of Calais*)

In 1891, when Rodin received from the Société des Gens de Lettres the commission for a sculpture of Balzac to be placed in front of the Palais Royal, he had little idea how prophetic his remark to his patrons would be: "I should like to do something out of the ordinary."[17] After the final plaster version of the sculpture was exhibited seven years later, it could safely be said that neither the public's image of Balzac, the Société des Gens de Lettres, nor Rodin would ever be the same again. Today the occasional alert passerby at the juncture of the Boulevard Raspail and Boulevard Montparnasse in Paris, and the crowds in the Sculpture Garden of The Museum of Modern Art in New York, still look with mixed feelings on Rodin's last monumental work, though unaware of the furor raised by its first showing. Probably no other modern sculpture continues to evoke such indecision and violent feeling as to its success or failure.

p. 99

The artist himself regarded this as his most important and daring work, "the sum of my whole life, result of a whole lifetime of effort, the mainspring of my esthetic theory. From the day of its conception, I was a changed man."[18] Yet, in 1898, although supported by many friendly writers and critics against what seemed the entire public, a predominantly hostile press, and his patrons themselves, Rodin on at least one occasion confided that perhaps he should have dropped the project three years earlier. In another instance, his correspondence reveals that he considered the adverse reception of the sculpture a bitter defeat. At other times, he consoled himself that the *Balzac* could be appreciated only by connoisseurs. The ambivalence of the artist's own reaction is all the more fascinating because, even though he generally seems to have regarded this as his masterpiece, he never attempted to carry his ideas in the *Balzac* further in other large-scale works. This suggests that he may have come to feel that, with this sculpture, he had reached a limit beyond which he could not, or would not, trespass. Possibly he may have exhausted his quantum of courage and had no more with which to confront the public with a new work on the heroic scale of the *Balzac*. In spite of an offer from a wealthy Belgian, and the artist's own considerable financial means after 1900, this sculpture was never cast in bronze during his lifetime.[19]

In his first contract with his patrons, Rodin agreed to deliver the monument within eighteen months, in January 1893. Possibly he thought he could build upon the incomplete sketch of a seated *Balzac* which had been commissioned from Chapu, who had died in 1891. Emile Zola, president of the literary society, successfully championed Rodin as Chapu's successor for this unfinished memorial. Rodin immediately discovered, however, that neither Chapu's work nor earlier portraits by David d'Angers would suffice. Balzac had died in 1850; the sculptor was faced with the challenge of re-creating both a likeness and a personality with which he had no first-hand contact, but which survived in the

Heads: Studies for the "Monument to Balzac."
1892–95. Above: left, plaster, 17″ high;
right, terra cotta and plaster, 8¼″ high;
Left: terra cotta, 9¼″ high.

Opposite: above, wax, 8¼″ high;
below, plaster, 7½″ high

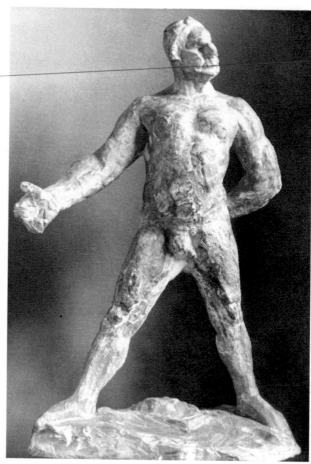

Two Studies for Balzac. Left: *Balzac, Clothed.* 1892–95. Plaster, 23⅝″ high. Right: *Balzac, Nude.* 1893. Bronze, 17¾″ high

92

public mind and eye through writings, photographs and portraits by painters as well as by caricaturists. Although still at work on a monument to Victor Hugo and involved with the final details of *The Burghers of Calais*, Rodin set out with typical avidity and thoroughness to increase his reading of Balzac's works and, guided by the writer Octave Mirbeau, to find the best descriptions of his subject. The Musée Rodin possesses two books on Balzac by Werdet and Lamartine, with passages that graphically analyze the writer's appearance marked by the artist.[20]

In the firm belief that the geographical area in which a man was born would reveal similar ethnic types, and that physical environment could influence character, Rodin beginning in 1891 made lengthy trips into Balzac's home territory around Tours. He made actual clay sketches of Tourangeaux whose resemblance to the dead man struck him. Balzac's old tailor was commissioned to make a suit of clothes to the measurement that he had kept throughout the years. In Paris, Rodin encountered a factory worker who seemed to possess the author's features, which he then transposed into wax and clay studies. Over forty studies in wax, clay, plaster and bronze have survived, but they have so far resisted complete dating or the establishment of a firm chronology.[21] These studies, however, indicate the triple nature of Rodin's problem. First was the task of recreating the head—the likeness that would mirror the spirit. Second, the body had to be built and the amount of stress to accord it be decided. Third, should the figure be clothed, and if so, how?

At the outset, the artist indicated that obtaining a resemblance was not his major problem: "I think of his intense labor, of the difficulty of his life, of his incessant battles and of his great courage. I would express all that."[22] Statements such as this suggest that Rodin may have identified himself with Balzac, so that the projected portrait was in some sense a double one. As the enormity of his objective unfolded in his imagination, Rodin's studies increased, but so did his inactivity, due to demands upon his health and creative powers. Deadlines were continually protracted. His despair deepened as it alternated with moments of enthusiasm.[23] Many of the portrait heads have a workmanlike quality, as if the *p. 90, 91* artist were assembling the characteristic features—the great brows, disheveled hair, protruding lips, upturned moustache and fleshy nose. Some expressions appear contrived in order to test the appropriateness of stressing the diabolic or the garrulous. In the wax head in the Pollak collection, one senses that Rodin *p. 91* was truly inspired by working from a living model. The features work together, flowing over a firm cranial structure; for instance, the ridge of the right cheek begins back near where the ear would be and continues until it merges with the nostrils and the profile. It is one of the sensuous studies of the series, for flesh has been given both weight and mobility. The face with its symmetry of brows and jowls operates with an incessant fluidity against the implied stability of the cube formed by the entire head. The man is alive with a masculine alertness coupled with an air of subtly detached knowing.

Bust of Balzac. 1893–95. Bronze, 18¼″ high

Probably naked and clothed figure studies alternated, although in the first years the latter preceded. At that time, Balzac's penchant for always appearing relaxed suggested to Rodin a slouched, seated figure with arms crossed (a cast is in the Rodin Museum, Philadelphia); in another version of the same pose, the

p. 92

clothed writer leans casually against a support with a pile of books nearby. Recognizing the triteness of rendering the prolific nature of Balzac's mind by a stack of books, Rodin thereafter concentrated his efforts on making the body and head heroic, without loss of their unique identity. A passage that he under-lined in Werdet's biography refers to the "courageous athlete." The strongest

p. 92

nude study of 1893, and possibly the finest sculpture of the entire series, gives Balzac the wide open, pugnacious stance of a wrestler. The power and expres-siveness of this conception reside in its successive support of tangible weights: the spread muscular legs sustain the massive torso, with its glorious bulging stomach, and the torso in turn supports the large but deceptively soft arms; the neck is the right thickness for the massive head. Either before or after this study, Rodin did the bust alone, from the folded arms up, and gave it some of the most inspired modeling in the series. The forward tilt of the head is accentuated more than in the full-figure version, creating a forceful counterweight to the thrust of the arms and giving to the whole a less militant, more reflective mood.

Following these sketches chronologically, in all likelihood, is the headless

94   Opposite: *Study for Balzac, Nude.* 1893–95. Bronze, 50¼″ high

muscular torso with the left hand holding the right forearm, exhibited in the chapel of the Musée Rodin.[24] Seen from the front, the crossed hands conceal the groin; looked at from the right side, the figure's right hand appears to have a firm grip on the penis. Perhaps Frank Harris had seen this sculpture in Rodin's studio and had it in mind when he wrote of a later version of the *Balzac:* "Under the old monastic robe with its empty sleeves the man holds himself erect, the hands firmly grasping his virility and the head thrown back."[25] Possibly Rodin hit upon this gesture when he first conceived the idea of showing Balzac as having brought his own world into being. In a second version of the headless torso, Rodin raised the right hand, divesting it of its sexual implications; but even after the artist began to cover the torso with the greatcoat or bathrobe that both he and Balzac liked to wear, the basic gesture of the arms and hands remains, as does the stance with weight carried on the rear foot.

Study for Balzac's Robe. 1893–95. Terra cotta, 13¾" high

It has been suggested that Rodin's *Balzac* was influenced by sculptures of Medardo Rosso, or that his inspiration for robing the figure came from a Japanese figurine of a monk given him by an English admirer.[26] Though both are possible sources, they are neither probable nor necessary, and in this case the question of influence on Rodin has been magnified beyond true importance. One must look at the whole long series to see how slowly and naturally Balzac's posture and the position of his limbs evolved, rather than resulting from a sudden decision made after Rodin had seen another work of art. As early as 1892, he had tried clothing Balzac in his "Dominican frock." In a recorded conversation with one of his secretaries before 1906, he referred to his decision to adopt the robe:

> The dress of the Roman was universal and for all time, in this sense, that it did not mar the beauty of the human body. This is also true of much of the clothing of the Middle Ages. That is why I did not strip Balzac; because, as you know, his habit of working in a sort of dressing gown *(houppelande)* gave me the opportunity of putting him into a loose flowing robe that supplied me with good lines and profiles without dating the statue.[27]

96

The sculptor's experience with the drapery of *The Burghers* during these same years would also have given him a relevant source and incentive for clothing the sculpture.

What Rodin meant by "good lines" is understandable when the final full-scale *Balzac* is seen on its high pedestal against the sky, from a point below and *p. 100* at a distance. The robe's folds, edges and sleeves concertedly sweep the eye up to the head. The drapery of the *Balzac*, unlike that of *The Burghers*, is not as insistent in its demands upon the viewer's attention. The fierce shadow accents of *The Burghers'* drapery are lacking in the *houppelande*, and the most expressive concentration of blacks has been reserved for the head. Rodin described the mode of the *Balzac* as one in which he had been able to simplify the major

Headless Nude Torso:
Study for Balzac. 1893–95.
Plaster, 37¾" high

97

Monument to Balzac. 1897. Above: *Final Small-Scale Study.* Plaster,
41¾″ high. Opposite: *Final Enlarged Version.* Plaster, 118″ high

planes in accordance with the sculpture's location and the remote prospects from which it was to be seen. The silhouettes are less complex and varied than those of *The Burghers*; the sculptor wanted the *Balzac* to be seen only from three or four advantageous standpoints.

In the chapel of the Musée Rodin stand side by side the final four-foot-high *p. 98* model of *Balzac* that Rodin finished with his own hands, and the full-scale *p. 99* version that his assistants had enlarged by the pointing method for him to exhibit. Unquestionably Rodin also worked on the latter, for certain small changes are evident. In some ways this juxtaposition of the two sculptures is unfortunate for the larger work. At close range, the smaller work seems to possess more concentrated power and greater spontaneity and freshness in execution, particularly in the areas of the face and the left sleeve; while the full-scale plaster by contrast appears somewhat rubbery and air inflated, the modeling over-reticent to the point of being inert and in spots uneventful. Rodin seems to have tried to iron out of the larger work many of the irregularities and rough spots that today seem to have given fire to the smaller one. To gain an effect of over-all grandeur in his work when seen from a distance, Rodin chose to sacrifice some of its vigorous modeling and expressiveness when seen intimately in a small area.

From a few feet away, the head of the large *Balzac* may still strike some viewers as it did in 1898, as a gross caricature of the writer.[28] Although the features are brutally reduced to an untempered sequence of lumps and hollows, the head can only be that of Balzac. The accumulated knowledge and finesse of the preceding portraits were somehow distilled, or suppressed and rejected in one *p. 90, 91* bold cast of the dice. To replace this head with any other in the series would have been to undermine the esthetic and conceptual unity of the whole. Rodin had achieved the sculptural equivalent of Lamartine's inspired description:

> It was the face of an element; big head, hair dishevelled over his collar and cheeks, like a wave which the scissors never clipped; very obtuse; eye of flame; colossal body. He was big, thick, square at the base and shoulders, with much of the ampleness of Mirabeau, but no heaviness. There was so much soul that it carried that lightly; the weight seemed to give him force, not to take it away from him; his short arms gesticulated with ease.[29]

The side views of the *Balzac* enforce its sexuality. Rodin has transformed the embattled writer into a godlike visionary who belongs on a pedestal aloof from the crowd. His head has become a fountainhead of creative power, and by a kind of Freudian upward displacement it continues the sexual emphasis of the earlier headless nude study. What more fitting tribute to Balzac's potency as a *p. 97* creator from the sculptor most obsessed with the life force! To enhance the tribute, Rodin dreamed of having his sculpture cut in dark granite not unlike Egyptian Pharaonic statues and the great stele of the Code of Hammurabi in the Louvre.[30] The big plaster, withdrawn from exhibition at the Salon of 1898

Opposite: *Monument to Balzac*. 1897. Bronze, 111″ high

because of the uproar, was subsequently removed to Rodin's home at Meudon outside of Paris. Lovingly he studied it there by moonlight, and it was thus that

p. 104, 193 Edward Steichen made the memorable photographs which Rodin believed captured what he had intended to show. Against the moonlight, *Balzac* seems to walk alone through the night.

From the moment of the first exhibition of his work, there is evidence that the artist was not completely satisfied with it and would have preferred to have kept it longer from the public:

> I should prefer to contemplate it every day for a while, and wait until a sudden inspiration, such as occasionally flashes through the brain, came to flood my imagination and enable me to perfect and idealize my work. For a work, even when achieved, is never perfect; it is always susceptible to a modification that can increase its beauty. [31]

Until Rodin's atelier notes are published, it is not possible to say whether Rodin actually did modify the statue, which remained in his possession from the time it was removed from exhibition until his death.

The scope and savagery of the public attack upon the *Monument to Balzac* shocked even the already battle-scarred artist. One can gauge the magnitude of the virulent attack by the fact that it could not be diminished or overshadowed in the press by the Dreyfus Affair – with which the *Balzac* became indirectly involved. Much to the dismay of many of Dreyfus' supporters, who numerically were the majority of those who stood by Rodin in the *Balzac* dispute, the artist felt that to declare himself for Dreyfus would have distracted further from an honest assessment of his work.

Even before the *Balzac*'s display, the press had been filled with reports of what it would look like and of the patrons' dismay over its progress. In view of this adverse prejudgment, it is not surprising that on the day before the opening of the Salon the President of the Republic, Félix Faure, escorted through the hall by Rodin, snubbed the *Balzac* by turning his back upon it and lavishing all his comment upon the marble version of *The Kiss* set up nearby. Ironically, Rodin had decided to exhibit the latter in order to educate the public in the direction and development of his art, to demonstrate what he had learned about the importance of suppressing detail in favor of the silhouette, and to provide a model for younger sculptors to follow:

> Undoubtedly the intertwining of *The Kiss* is pretty, but in this group I made no discovery. It is a theme treated according to the academic tradition, a sculpture complete in itself and artificially set apart from the surrounding world. My *Balzac*, on the contrary, by its pose and look makes one imagine the milieu in which he walked, lived and thought. He is inseparable from his surroundings. He is like a veritable living being. The same was true earlier with my *Walking Man*. The interest lies not in the figure itself, but rather in the thought of the stage he has passed through and the one through which he is about to move. This art that by suggestion goes beyond the model requires the imagination to recompose the work when it is seen from close up. [32]

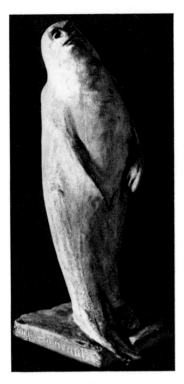

Seal Posed as Balzac. 1898?
Plaster, 9¼″ high

The presence of the slick, impeccably carved marble *Kiss* gave former friends the chance to argue that while Rodin had been right in the past, he had since lost his way or burnt himself out with the *Balzac*. He was accused variously of having depicted his subject as a penguin, a snowman, a sack of coal, a menhir, a phantom, a colossal fetus and a shapeless larva.[33] Other criticisms included the charge that Balzac had been reduced to the role of an actor in a gigantic Guignol, that he had just gotten out of bed to confront a creditor, or that exposing the public to such maladroit handling of proportions and physical distortion was equivalent to the dangers of a live bomb. For some, the *Balzac* was a symbol of the aberrations of *fin-de-siècle* mentality, while the more charitable claimed that it possessed "too much philosophy and not enough modeling." That Rodin appeared to be mocking the public seemed to many to justify the small plaster caricatures of the sculpture that were made and sold on the streets of Paris. One of these in the Rodin Museum at Philadelphia shows a seal in the position of *Balzac*; on its base is written "One Step Forward," a jesting reference both to the pose and to the notion of Rodin's leadership in sculpture.

The decision of the Société des Gens de Lettres to dishonor their contract and refuse the work was arrived at on the basis that they could not recognize Balzac in this "crude sketch." To this Rodin replied:

Without doubt the decision of the Société is a material disaster for me, but my work as an artist remains my supreme satisfaction. I am anxious to recover the peace and tranquility of which I have need. I sought in *Balzac*, as in *Victor Hugo*, to render in sculpture what was not photographic. One can find errors in my *Balzac*; the artist does not always realize his dream; but I believe in the truth of my principle; and *Balzac*, rejected or not, is none the less in the line of demarcation between commercial sculpture and the art of sculpture that we no longer have in Europe. My principle is to imitate not only form but also life. I search in nature for this life and amplify it by exaggerating the holes and lumps, to gain thereby more light, after which I search for a synthesis of the whole…. I am now too old to defend my art, which has sincerity as its defense. The taste of the public has been tainted by the habit of making casts after the model, to which it has grown accustomed.[34]

Edward Steichen. *"Balzac" – The Silhouette, 4 a.m.* 1908. Pigment print

1. "Liberty, in a breastplate of brass, cleaving the air with unfolded wings, roars in a mighty voice, 'Aux armes, citoyens!' She raises high her left arm to rally all the brave to her side, and, with the other hand, she points her sword towards the enemy. It is she, beyond question, whom you first see, for she dominates all the work, and her legs, which are wide apart as if she were running, seem like an accent placed above the sublime war-epic. It seems as though one must hear her–for her mouth of stone shrieks as though to burst your eardrum. But no sooner has she given the call than you see the warriors rush forward. This is the second phase of the action. A Gaul with the mane of a lion shakes aloft his helmet as though to salute the goddess, and here, at his side, is his young son, who begs the right to go with him–'I am strong enough, I am a man, I want to go!' he seems to say, grasping the hilt of a sword. 'Come,' says the father, regarding him with tender pride.

"Third phase of the action: a veteran bowed beneath the weight of his equipment strives to join them–for all who have strength enough must march to battle. Another old man, bowed with age, follows the soldiers with his prayers, and the gesture of his hand seems to repeat the counsels that he has given them from his own experience.

"Fourth phase: an archer bends his muscular back to bind on his arms. A trumpet blares its frenzied appeal to the troops. The wind flaps the standards, the lances point forward. The signal is given, and already the strife begins" (On Art and Artists, pp. 98-100).

2. Copies of Rodin's letters to the Calais committee can be found in the Free Library of Philadelphia, on microfilm in the Library of The Museum of Modern Art, and in photostat in the Fine Arts Library of Indiana University. See also the chapter on The Burghers of Calais in Cladel, Rodin, New York, Harcourt, Brace, 1937.

3. The letter is dated November 20, 1884.

4. This letter is undated.

5. Lawton, op. cit., p. 162.

6. Letter dated December 8, 1893.

7. Undated letter.

8. Article by Croze, Echo de Paris, June 1, 1895.

9. Letter dated December 8, 1893.

10. Letter to Mayor Dewavrin, July 14, 1885.

11. On Art and Artists, pp. 103-04.

12. Undated letter.

13. Undated letter.

14. Cladel, Rodin, p. 100.

15. Frisch and Shipley, op. cit., p. 203.

16. Cladel, op. cit., p. 91.

17. L. Scholl, article in Echo de Paris, August 28, 1896.

18. Cladel, op. cit., p. 145 and the entire chapter on the Monument to Balzac.

19. Ibid., p. 158. It was not until 1939 that a committee formed for the purpose succeeded in having the work publicly installed in Paris.

20. Cécile Goldscheider provides documentary material on the Balzac in two articles ("La Genèse d'une oeuvre, Le Balzac de Rodin," Bulletin Esthétique, vol. LV, 1951, pp. 201-03; "La Genèse d'une oeuvre, Le Balzac de Rodin," Revue des Arts, vol. 11, 1952, pp. 37-44) and an exhibition catalogue (Balzac et Rodin, Paris, Musée Rodin, 1950). In the later article, she cites the existence of these two biographies in the library of the Musée Rodin; as they were not made available for this study, it was not possible to see all the passages marked by Rodin.

21. Goldscheider, Balzac et Rodin. Leo Steinberg has stated that on a visit to the Meudon studio in the summer of 1962, he found among the terra cottas in one of the glass cases what he believes to be a small study for the Balzac. This study, of which no photographs exist in the albums of the Musée Rodin, does not appear in Goldscheider's writings on the subject.

22. Cladel, op. cit., p. 131, gives the whole letter.

23. Many writers commented upon Rodin's extreme illness and prolonged fatigue during the year 1894-95.

24. Cladel, op. cit., p. 126.

25. Frank Harris, Contemporary Portraits, London, 1915, vol. I.

26. Mme Goldscheider believes in the latter possibility, but does not know at what date the figurine was given to Rodin (see Revue des Arts, loc. cit., fig. 16). A more interesting suggestion is that the backward slant of Balzac's stance was influenced by works of Medardo Rosso, for whom Rodin is known to have professed great admiration. For a discussion of the relations between the two men, see Margaret Scolari Barr's forthcoming monograph on Rosso, to be published by The Museum of Modern Art.

27. Ludovici, op. cit., p. 112.

28. Henri Rochefort complained in an article that "no one has ever thought of extracting a man's brain and putting it upon his face" (Cladel, op. cit., p. 143).

29. Quoted in Lawton, op. cit., p. 179.

30. Cladel, op. cit., p. 158. I am indebted to Professor Steve Marcus of Columbia University for his observations on the sexual imagery.

31. Lawton, op. cit. (New York edition), p. 119.

32. La Revue, November 1, 1907, p. 105.

33. Detailed accounts of the reaction to the Monument to Balzac are given by Cladel, op. cit., and the article "Rodin" in Larousse, Grand Encyclopédie, 1918 edition.

34. The article, signed "X," appeared in Journal (Paris), May 12, 1898.

The Man with the Broken Nose. 1863–64. Bronze, 9½″ high

THE PORTRAITS

FOR THE PSYCHOLOGICAL CHALLENGE that it presented, Rodin esteemed the portrait above all other subjects. "To tell the truth, there is no artistic work which requires as much penetration as the bust and the portrait."[1] There was no doubt in his mind that in a portrait bust he could create the equivalent of his subject's whole biography, the period in which he lived, his ethnic origin, profession, psychology and personal character. His portraits made permanent the look and spirit of men and women from the arts and letters, business and politics, and every step on the social scale, from a handyman with battered face to the élite of several continents. Everyman was potentially the subject for his art. "Nature is always beautiful.... You speak of a face without expression. There is no such face to an artist... even the most insignificant head is the dwelling place of life."[2] For Rodin, there were no subjects without character, only art without character.

Like countless artists before him, Rodin was an avid amateur of physiognomy. The most succinct affirmation of his beliefs was his statement that the artist "has only to look into a human face in order to read there the soul within – not a feature deceives him."[3] In his eloquent comments on the sculptural portraits by other artists, Rodin assigned specific qualities, traits and habits to the lines, movement, direction and weight of the features: "The line of a forehead, the least lifting of a brow, the flash of an eye, reveal to him all the secrets of a heart."[4] Only rarely did he analyze one of his own portraits verbally, but his observations on Houdon's busts of Voltaire, Mirabeau and Benjamin Franklin reveal how he read the face.[5] They show how attentive Rodin was to the care or neglect of the sitter's hair and dress, the lift or sag of the head, the degree of inclination and the height of the forehead. The line of the brows and the angles formed by the eyebrows expressed character traits; and he particularly noticed the extent and type of the eyes' mobility, and the presence or absence of their focus. From the prominence of the cheekbones, length of the nose, protuberance and relative fullness of the mouth, weight and fall of the cheeks, and cut of the chin, Rodin reconstructed the profession, character and cultural background of Houdon's subjects. This reconstruction he then augmented by observing the set of the neck on the shoulders, and the formation of the chest and its proportion in relation to the whole body. (Barrel chests he felt were for orators.) A contracted face Rodin equated with miserliness, an expansive one with generosity. He liked to differentiate his sitters and those of other artists according to Latin and Nordic ethnic types. He also practiced a kind of comparative phys-

107

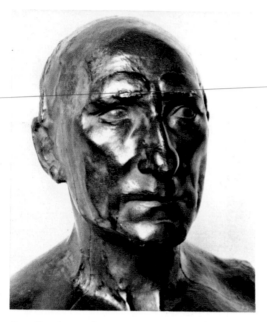

Jean-Baptiste Rodin, the Artist's Father. 1860.
Gilded bronze, 16⅛" high

Right: *Père Pierre-Julien Eymard.* 1863.
Bronze, 23½" high

iognomy between human beings and animals; the bust he had made of Falguière he compared to a "little bull," and he saw in Titian's portrait of Pope
Paul III the "snout of a marten."[6] Associations of this kind prevent us from
taking too literally Rodin's insistence that he sought to render only what he
saw in his subject.

EARLY BUSTS

When late in Rodin's lifetime his early busts of his father and of Père Pierre-
Julien Eymard were exhibited, they caused considerable surprise and a favorable
reaction. The public and critics were unaccustomed to the ascetic hardness and
the cool precision with which he had achieved likeness in these beginning efforts. The power of the heads is generated largely by the force of the cranium,
over which the skin seems tautly pulled. In spite of his sentimental attachment
to both these men, Rodin preferred to show them in a detached way and limited
himself to the accurate recording of their anatomy, which alone gives them a
moving presence.[7] In neither work are the eyes and mouth treated as dramatically expressive. More moving are the large, deceptively smooth, continuous
areas of the brows and cheeks, and the compact silhouettes that emphasize the
emotional restraint of each figure. The precocious modeling and rigid, blocklike
frontality of these heads indicate that Rodin had matured as a craftsman before
he attained maturity as a person. The multifaceted aspects of human personality,
and the consequent need to develop the means of translating them more fully
in sculptural terms, had not yet been realized in the young artist's conciousness.
The young Rodin, an ardent admirer of Houdon, was demonstrating technical
lessons well learned.

"THE MAN WITH THE BROKEN NOSE"

The most famous and important of Rodin's early portraits is that of *The Man*   *p. 106*
with the Broken Nose, which in its plaster version he attempted unsuccessfully to
exhibit in a Salon of 1864 under that title. (This first plaster has been lost through
the casting of successive moulds.) The original terra cotta had frozen in Rodin's
unheated studio, so that its rear portion fell away. The plaster and the first
bronze cast were thus made from what had accidentally become a fragment,
with the back of the head missing; it was referred to by Rodin as a mask. Rodin
had selected for his model a neighborhood odd-job man named Bibi, because
he was attracted by the man's picturesque, battered face (and not, as has been
stated elsewhere, out of a desire to redo Roman Republican portraiture). About
1887, in his reminiscences to the American sculptor, Truman H. Bartlett, Rodin
said of *The Man with the Broken Nose*:

He had a fine head; belonged to a fine race – in form – no matter if he was brutalized. It was made as a piece of sculpture solely, and without reference to character of model, as such. I called it "The Broken Nose," because the face of the model was broken. That mask determined all my future work. It is the first good piece of modeling I ever did. From that time I sought to look all around my work, to draw it well in every respect. I have kept that mask before my mind in everything I have done. I tried it on my first figure, "The Bacchante," but it did not succeed; I again tried it on "The Age of Brass" (*sic*), also without succes, though it was a good figure. In fact I never succeeded in making a figure as good as "The Broken Nose."[8]

Many years after this plaster head had been rejected by the Salon of 1864, Rodin, in a somewhat malicious frame of mind, had a second version carved in marble. In this, the local handy-man Bibi was disguised as an ancient Roman senator and submitted to the Salon jury. With the dignified title of *Mr. B—*, it was accepted, although artistically it is inferior to the bronze.

Rodin gave to the original version an unselfconscious pathos through the inclination of the head, thus throwing the still-unanimated eyes into shadow. Contrary to the customary practice of providing shoulders and part of the chest, only a small area of the neck was shown, so that focus was directed almost exclusively to the face. In subsequent bronze versions of *The Man with the*

The Little Man with the Broken Nose. 1882.
Bronze, 5″ high

Broken Nose, the head is held erect. (The sculpture has suffered through the loss of the mould of the earliest cast.) The artist's own words make it clear that the angle of a head and movement were vital to portraiture:

> This is so even in my busts, to which I have often given a certain slant, a certain obliquity, a certain expressive direction, which would emphasize the meaning of the physiognomy.... The illusion of life is obtained in our art by good modeling and by movement. These two qualities are like the blood and the breath of all good work.[9]

The image of this broken-faced man persisted in Rodin's memory, as he has told us; and around 1882 he made a third version, some five inches high, which he inserted in the row of heads on the lintel over *The Thinker* in *The Gates of Hell*. When this last effort is compared with its prototype, it may at first appear that Rodin was simply showing the model twenty years older. The smaller head is moving, however, not because of the model's age, but because of the artist's greatly increased ability to re-create the face of an older man. The features are no longer isolated as individual elements. The sculpture has more unity; instead of being readable from part to part, eye, brow and cheek overlap or intrude into one another. Similarly, the characterization itself resists simple definition. Rodin was certainly as much interested in good modeling as he had been eighteen years before; but now, every inch of the surface is as eventful in biographical as it is in sculptural terms. By this time, Rodin was confirmed in his belief that art could and should express moral sentiments without didactic moralizing. The head of the old man is an image of the onset of death; the inconstant, weary flesh is an accounting of the toll that life exacts from those who live it hard. To have added a body to either of the heads would have been superfluous, for the area between chin and hairline was sufficient in which to present fully and dramatically a man's whole life.

PORTRAITS OF WOMEN

None of the many women who benefited from Rodin's talents as portraitist could claim to have had a finer portrait than Rose Beuret. His bust of her ("*Mignon*") was made shortly after their meeting in 1864. As Jean Charbonneau has wryly commented, the artist was so wedded to the sculpture that he could marry Rose herself only a few days before her death in 1917. Rodin never made a more frank and informal bust than that of his young mistress. Like Bernini's *Costanza Buonarelli*, it possesses inner fire. His later, more sedate portraits of elegant society women, such as *Miss Eve Fairfax*, lack its dashing quality and its sense of intimacy shared by subject and artist. The alert, erect head is framed by the energetic spiraling hair, accentuated and expressive in a way that is rare in Rodin's work. The hollowing of the iris that Rodin may have learned from Houdon or baroque sculptors such as Bernini, coupled with the parted lips, induces a dramatic expectancy that never recurs in his formal feminine por-

p. 112

p. 113

Mignon (Rose Beuret). 1870. Plaster, 15¾" high

Miss Eve Fairfax. c. 1905. Marble, 21⅝" high

traits. Throughout their life together, Rodin was to make innumerable studies of Rose Beuret, one of which served as the head of the winged spirit in *The Call to Arms*. Seeing her on her death bed, the old sculptor remarked how much she resembled a fine sculpture. *p. 68*

Rodin had a far greater reserve about showing women's faces than their bodies. That he felt no such inhibition about revealing what he saw in men is evident from what he told an assistant:

> In portraits of our own sex, we must pierce without pity the innermost crannies of their souls, must strip them of disguise, lay bare the intemperate, even vicious passions that surge in them daily.... But a portrait of a woman is another thing, their nature is not ours, we are far from grasping it; we must therefore be respectful and discreet. We must be circumspect in unveiling their tender and delicate mystery. Even with them, always the truth, but not always all the truth. Sometimes we may, just a little, drop the veil. [10]

This, however, was the old Rodin speaking, not the passionate young artist who modeled the youthful bust of Rose.

Typical of Rodin's developed style in feminine portraits is the wax bust of *Mrs. Russell*, done before 1888. Wax was his preferred medium for such works *p. 114*

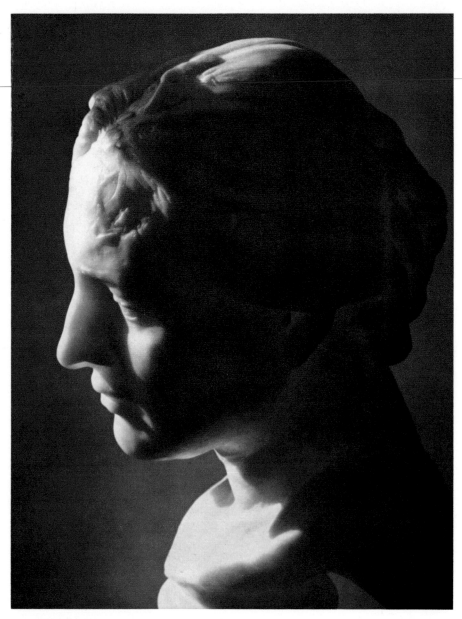

Mrs. Russell. Before 1888. Wax, 18½″ high

Thought (Camille Claudel). 1886. Marble, 29½" high × 17" wide × 18" deep

because it directly caught the lightness and warmth of woman's flesh. This bust represents what might be called the artist's idealized cosmetic mode, in which for the most part he preserves the beauty of unblemished skin and draws out the property the medium exhibits, under light, of imparting a soft translucency to the surface. The delicate surface treatment matches the subject's quiet revery. (The passionate women in Rodin's art are anonymous—models, or those who could not afford portraits but agreed to pose in the nude for his figure studies.) Unlike Medardo Rosso, with whom he is often compared, Rodin never suppressed by understatement the protrusions and recessions of a woman's head. In *Mrs. Russell,* he avoided blacks and sharp edges but found a subtle scale of fluid shadow modulations to play off against the dominant blondness of the flesh. His sculptures of women, far more than those of men, require a sympathetic lighting to reveal fully the extremely gentle faceting of a brow or cheekbone that prevents an excessively liquid effect.

p. 115 One of Rodin's portraits of Camille Claudel, the talented young sculptress who was his mistress for many years, shows her head emerging from a rough block of stone. Calling it *Thought,* the sculptor later said that he was curious to see if through the lifelike modeling of the head and the suggestions given by the pose (and, in all probability, the associations with the title), he could not make the viewer imagine the circulation of blood even within the uncut stone block. By showing a disembodied head, he may have sought to represent it as the locus of consciousness, or to convey the idea that during revery there is no awareness of the body.

A more interesting and less didactic experiment, from the present-day point of view, was Rodin's enormous enlargement of the originally small *Head of Iris,* made from one of his models.[11] The heads that he made for his own pleasure differ from his commissioned portraits in marble by their looser, more informal modeling, greater psychological inquisitiveness and deeper penetration into the range of feminine moods. The *Large Head of Iris,* blown up from its original scale to over twice life-size with apparently little or no change in modeling, has no precedent among previous heads in either painting or sculpture. It is Rodin's most awesome, mysterious and frightening head, the one most susceptible to poetic interpretation. This is a rare instance in which deformity derives not from the model, but from the sculptor. Effort is required, not to feel the power, but to rationalize the formal beauty of a head that at first seems bloated and without form. Paradoxically, the very grossness demands the most exquisite and thoughtful modeling, a consummate knowledge of the myriad nuances of which a head is capable. The head appears to grow from the coarse, massive neck which sustains its weight and quality. The immutable set of the eyes and the scarlike mouth, together with the shape of the head set like a dolmen on its bulky support, impart an ironic heroicism and defiant spirit. The face looks as if wars might have been waged upon it. No small area readily translates itself

Large Head of Iris. 1890–91. Bronze, 23⅝″ high

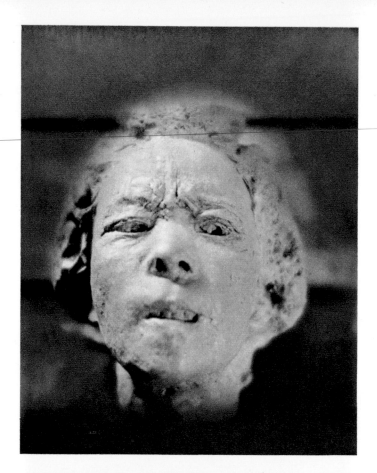

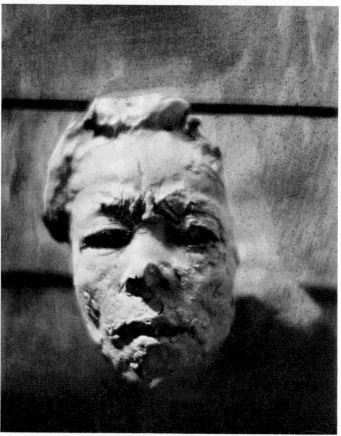

118

into a facial feature, and each part is predictable only on the basis of the whole. Even more than *The Helmet-Maker's Wife*, the *Large Head of Iris* is Rodin's p. 64, 65 proof that the beauty of art resides in its making. It may be his most haunting sculpture for our time.

Between 1908 and 1911, Rodin made several portraits of a diminutive Japanese dancer named Hanako, who was performing in Paris. The resulting series of heads was unprecedented in either Western or Eastern sculpture as a revelation of the changes that can be enacted upon one woman's face. The series gains additional interest in the choice of a woman whose culture and training had taught her facial control and the masking of feeling, but whose mask disintegrated under the sculptor's searching inquiry. Edward Steichen, who had been given permission to photograph Rodin's works as he pleased, with rare understanding made photographs of two clay studies of Hanako. By his choice of angle, lighting and intimate distance, Steichen photographed them as if they were the living person, so that one's first confrontation suggests that his pictures are of the woman herself. Here one can see the occasions on which Rodin "dropped the veil" with which he usually discreetly protected his feminine subjects. So intense was his concentration on the model that he retained her optical squint. He preserved the mobility of Hanako's face, seen in con-

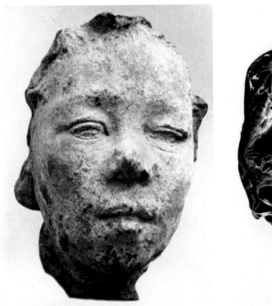 

Opposite: Edward Steichen. *Rodin's "Hanako."* 1908. Pigment prints. Above: left, *Hanako*. 1908. Bronze, 7″ high. Above: right, *Japanese Head (Hanako)*. 1908. Gilded bronze, 6½″ high

119

trasting moments – of quiet discourse, and of teeth-clenched fury. In the former, a curious effect of aging has been caused by notations made with small pieces of clay, and knife cuts on the eyelid – not smoothed over, but left as a precious record of a sculpture in progress, with all the decisions and problems still bared to the eye. In the other, one can only marvel at Rodin's response to the mouth. It is possible that the angry expression of this consummately trained actress may have come from Kabuki repertory or a Khmer pose, rather than from instinct. But such contrived expressions, like the hieratic, ritualized gestures of the Cambodian dancers that he drew in 1906, would have intrigued Rodin, who hungered for a total knowledge of human behavior and for its possession through art. The brilliance of Steichen's photographs, which were taken in the artist's studio probably soon after the sculptures were made, also permit one to see the differences between a subject in the original clay and the later bronze version. While the bronze cast of the angry *Hanako* in the California Palace of the Legion of Honor seems close to the clay head, the warmth, color, softness and – for a brief period – moistness of the clay have resisted transposition into metal.

p. 167

p. 119

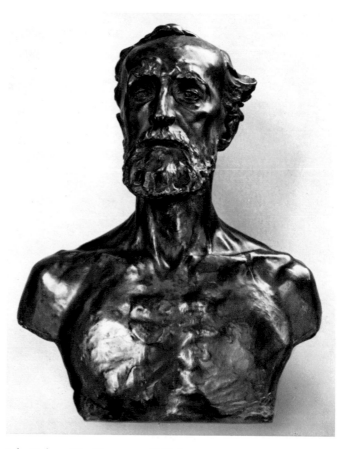

Jules Dalou. 1883. Bronze, 20¾" high

PORTRAITS OF MEN

The several portraits of writers and artists of the 1880s and '90s serve as reminders that at least in his friends Rodin had a small, sophisticated audience upon whom he could rely to receive his art sympathetically. (Usually, however, the sitter was the most displeased by the portrait.) In spite of his hermetic work habits, Rodin lived and worked in Paris throughout his life and after 1880 was accepted in the highest intellectual and social circles there. He even held audiences in his studio on Saturdays. His many notes of thanks to writers indicate that he read all the newspaper articles concerning his work. Greater maturity and contact with cultured Parisians may account for the change in Rodin's portrait style from his earlier eighteenth-century modes, severe and frivolous. His friendship, between 1880 and 1885, with most of the subjects–J.-P. Laurens, Alphonse Legros, Henri Becque, Maurice Haquette, Dalou and Carrier-Belleuse *p. 208* –may have encouraged him to achieve the frank and honest style he so cherished, and for which he was admired. It should, however, be pointed out that Rodin's portrait technique evolved concurrently with his figure style, so that individuality of appearance was insured in every representation. He explained his procedure in these words:

> In working on a bust, or in fact any figure, I always carefully model by profiles,
> not from a merely front view. It gives depth and solidity, the volume, in fine, and
> its location in space. I do this, however, with a line that starts from one's own
> brain. I mean that I note the deviations of the head from the oval type. In one the
> forehead bulges out over the rest of the face, in another, the lower jaw bulges out in
> contrast with the receding forehead. With this line of deviation established, I unite
> all the profiles, and thus get the lifelike form.... On beginning their work, they
> [the artists] should exaggerate characteristic features. The exaggerations are necessary
> to establish the structural expression. It is only by the graduation of these more
> characteristic traits that the relative value of all the parts can be determined. In
> the flesh, there is the spirit that magnifies one or another detail of expression. In
> the clay or marble, it must be by the positive magnifying of the material part,
> not especially by size, but by the line, by the direction, the depth, the length of its
> curve, that the expression is made equivalent. [12]

Rodin claimed that there was no face that lacked expression or betrayed the true nature of its owner's soul. While many of his sitters disagreed with the latter contention, none disputed the former.

Looked at together, however, Rodin's portraits of the 1880s exhibit certain uniform characteristics irrespective of their individuality in characterization. Generally, the head is frontal, held erect or thrust slightly forward. Though the amount of the chest shown may vary, the model is usually nude. In these heads, unlike those of *The Burghers of Calais* or *The Gates of Hell,* the range of facial expressions is extremely limited, with the variations confined to the habitual set of the eyes or mouth. There is an aura of grave formality, as if the artist were trying to portray his contemporaries as modern-day noble Romans. Once, in discussing the portrait of Rochefort, Rodin admitted that he sought the effect of a Roman emperor, adding, "I have never found the Latin classic type as pure as in Rochefort."[13] The bust of the academic painter of historical subjects, J.-P. Laurens, is another example of Rodin's habit of seeing his subject as the scion of an ancient ethnic group: "From the design of his skull, he was probably descended from the ancient Visigoths of Spain, and...this type was characterized by the prominence of the lower jaw."[14] (As a favor to Laurens, Rodin himself posed for one of the Merovingian warriors who assist at the death of St. Geneviève, in the Pantheon murals.)

p. 120   Rodin was responsive to the style of his subjects – for example, the aristocratic bearing of Jules Dalou, an intensely vain Communard who had been exiled and pardoned, and who, as Rodin saw it, aspired to a position comparable to that of Lebrun under Louis XIV. There was no living artist whom the sculptor held in greater veneration, amounting to awe, than Puvis de Chavannes. His dying words were in defense of Puvis' greatness. Rodin's respect for the painter

Puvis de Chavannes. 1910. Marble, 29¼" high × 49¼" wide × 23⅜" deep

Puvis de Chavannes. 1891. Bronze, 19¾″ high

was in fact so great that when Puvis begged that his naked chest in the clay bust be clothed, the portrait was given a coat a few hours before the opening of the Salon. In his stone portraits of Puvis, Rodin apotheosized his subject by showing a disembodied head, floating as if in mists. In speaking of the bronze version, with its haughty aloofness, Rodin said of Puvis: "He carried his head high. His skull, solid and round, seemed made to wear a helmet. His arched chest seemed accustomed to carry the breastplate. It was easy to imagine him at Pavia fighting for his honor by the side of Francis I."[15]

Victor Hugo received the most Olympian treatment. Rodin struggled with several versions of monuments to the writer, which at one time included three p. 209 Muses and a gigantic rock upon which Hugo was shown with arm outstretched, stilling the sound of waves so that he might hear the voices of inspiration. The sculptor had the courage and good taste to keep cutting away these accessories until he arrived at his best efforts, which were of the head alone. "Hugo had the p. 124 air of a Hercules; belonged to a great race. Something of a tiger, or an old lion. He had an immense animal nature. His eyes were especially beautiful and the most striking thing about him."[16]

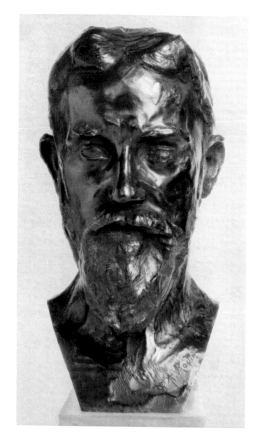

Victor Hugo. 1897. Bronze, 27½″ high

Right: *George Bernard Shaw.* 1906. Bronze, 15″ high

124

One of Rodin's strongest masculine portraits is that to which he gave the name of *Baudelaire*, but which was in fact made from a young artist. (This was not exceptional, for his portrait of *Gustav Mahler* was made from the sculptor's secretary, Mario Meunier, who bore a striking resemblance to the composer; while Mahler's likeness in turn inspired the bust of Mozart done in the following year.) The *Baudelaire* (of which there are at least two versions) parallels in time Rodin's work on the *Balzac*. In 1892 a group of writers for *La Plume*, including Leconte de Lisle and the Belgian artist, Félicien Rops, approached Rodin for a funerary monument to Baudelaire for the Montparnasse Cemetery. He immediately indicated that he did not want to do a full figure, and in the light of the decisions that he made later for the *Balzac*, his comments as recorded in a subsequent newspaper interview are interesting: "I cannot see a statue of Baudelaire. What is a statue after all; a body, arms, legs, covered with banal clothing. What do these have to do with Baudelaire, who lived only by his brain? With him, the head is everything." In the same interview, Rodin also spoke of the studies for the head in a way that shows how he wanted the portrait to be read:

p. 127

> It is not Baudelaire... but it is a head that resembles Baudelaire. There are a series of individual characteristics that, atavistically without a doubt, preserve the same cerebral conformation that constitutes what one calls the type; this bust is of a draftsman named Malteste who shows all the characteristic lines of the Baudelairean mask. See the enormous forehead, swollen at the temples, dented, tormented, handsome nevertheless, the face described at length by Cladel; the eyes have the look of disdain; the mouth is sarcastic, bitter in its sinuous line, but the swelling of the muscles, a little fat, announces his voluptuous appetites. In short, it is Baudelaire. [17]

Rodin resisted the idea of placing the head in a public location, saying that such sites were for generals, while *"Baudelaire* is too great a mystery for the mob." An old photograph showing Rodin at work on this head indicates that the face was turned up so that the fierce intensity of the gaze would not seem to be directed at any specific thing outside the head itself, in which there is a relentless interrogation of the features as extensions of the inner man.

None of the several portraits that Rodin made of George Bernard Shaw equals the force and beauty of the head of *Baudelaire*. This may have been because the language barrier did not allow Rodin an intimate acquaintance with Shaw's writings, discourse and personality. But although he could understand neither Shaw's English nor his attempts at French, he was impressed by his energy: "Mr. Shaw does not speak French well, but he is imposing by the vigorous manner with which he expresses himself." [18] One of the fortunate results of Shaw's sitting for Rodin was the writer's accounts of their sessions and the progress of the busts. Shaw was pleased and perhaps amused by the sculptor's likening of his face to that of Christ. The unbounded delight Shaw took in his effigies is transparent in his lengthy article on Rodin, written for the French newspaper *Gil Blas* on May 24, 1912. Twenty years later in another article, Shaw added some humorous and enlightening details of the artist's work habits that should preface the more serious early piece: "The most picturesque detail of his method was his taking a big draught of water into his mouth and spitting it onto the clay to keep it constantly pliable. Absorbed in his work, he did not always aim well and soaked my clothes."[19]

An excerpt from the long article follows:

In his very interesting book, *L'Art*, Rodin tells us that his marvelous portrait busts rarely pleased their models. I would go further and say that they astonish and disappoint the friends of the model. Look at these busts... and you will see the reason why. These are the busts of real men and not of celebrities' reputations. Look at my own bust and you will see no resemblance to that brilliant fiction known as George Bernard Shaw.... Moreover it is a frightening resemblance. It is that which really exists and not what one believes to exist. It is the same with Puvis de Chavannes as with all the others. Puvis de Chavannes protested, they say, by showing himself in a mirror and a photograph in order to prove that there was no resemblance to the bust. But I am convinced not only that he looked like his bust, but that his bust was really he as distinct from his stiff collars and public manners....

Rodin worked laboriously.... When he was uncertain he measured me with an old iron compass and then measured the bust. If the nose of the bust was too long he cut off a section and pressed the end to close the wound with no more emotion or affectation than a glazier replacing a window. If the ear was not in its place he would cut it off and lay it on correctly, these mutilations being executed cold-bloodedly in the presence of my wife (who almost expected to see the already terribly animated clay begin to bleed) while remarking that it was quicker to do it thusly than to make a new ear.

Moreover, while he worked he achieved a number of miracles. At the end of the first fifteen minutes, after having given a simple idea of the human form to the block of clay, he produced by the action of his thumb a bust so living that I would have taken it away with me to relieve the sculptor of any further work.... But this phase vanished like a summer cloud as the bust evolved. I say as the plan (design) evolved, because within the space of a month my bust passed successively, under my eyes, through all of the stages of art's evolution. The first fifteen minutes having passed, he became serious and began a careful reproduction of my features in their exact dimensions of life. Then, this representation went back mysteriously to the cradle of Christian art and, at this moment, I had the desire to say again: For the love of heaven, stop and give me that. It is truly a Byzantine masterpiece. Then, little by little it seemed that Bernini intermingled with the work. Then, to my great horror the bust softened in order to become a commendable eighteenth-century morceau, elegant enough to make one believe that Houdon had retouched a head by Canova or of Thorwaldsen.... Rodin himself studies his work with a hardened air.... Once again, a century rolled by in a single night, and the bust became a bust by Rodin and it was the living reproduction of the head that reposes on my shoulders. It was a process that seemed to belong to the study of an embryologist and not to an artist. The hand of Rodin worked, not as the hand of a sculptor works, but as the work of *Elan Vital*.... The Hand of God is his own hand....

126

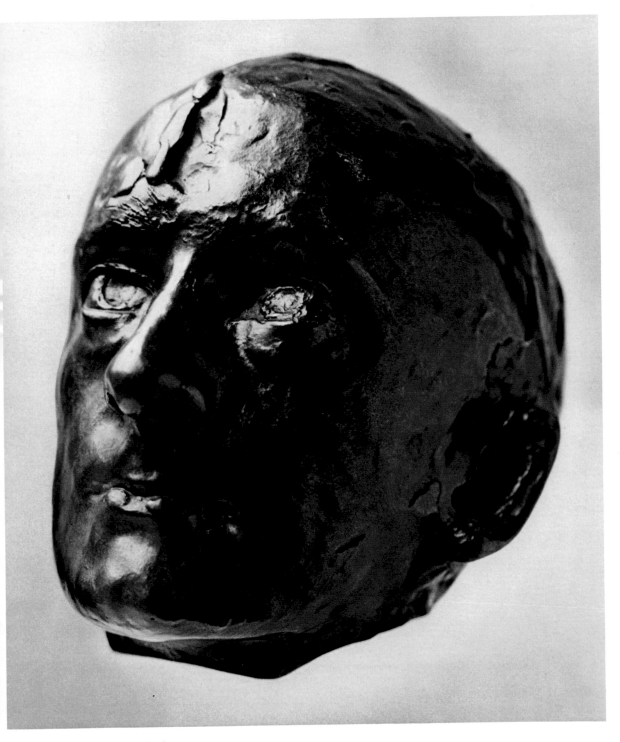

Baudelaire. 1898. Bronze, 8″ high

In his (personal) work he shows a highly developed feeling for the beauty of marble. He has given me three busts of myself: one in bronze, another in plaster and the last in marble. The bronze is me (when I was younger). The plaster is me. But the marble has a completely different type of life. It shines and the light emanates from it. It does not have the aspect of a solid: it has a luminous air and this éclat and extraordinary emanation prevent the curious from touching it. It seems in effect that one could not seize it. They pretend that all modern sculpture is made by Italian craftsmen who mechanically reproduce in stone the sculptor's plaster model. Rodin himself said it. But the particular qualities that Rodin obtains in his marbles are not in the clay models. While other sculptors may employ the same artisans employed by Rodin, none have produced marbles such as his. One day, Rodin told me that all modern sculpture is a fraud, that neither he nor any other sculptor knows how to use the chisel. A few days later he let fall this remark: "The manipulation of the chisel is amusing (strange)." Nevertheless, when he modelled a bust, his method is neither that of Michelangelo with his chisel, nor that of a modeller in his high relief but rather that of a draftsman who sketches in clay the thousand profiles that your head would present if it was cut through the center in a thousand sections from different angles....

In sum, outside of the manual skill that he shares with all who cut stone, he has only two qualities that make him the most divine worker that ever was. The first is a vision more profound and truly exact than that of the others. The second is a veracity and incorruptibility. And that is all, ladies and gentlemen. And now that I have told you his secret you can all become great sculptors. It is just as easy as any other manual work and much more agreeable, if you can acquire these two simple qualities.

To have one's portrait made by Rodin became the goal not only of the leaders of international society but also of European statesmen. They would have understood Shaw's praise: "Rodin has given me immortality, and biographical dictionaries in one thousand years from now will all contain the note: 'Shaw, George Bernard, subject of a bust by Rodin.' "[20] Shortly before the outbreak of the First World War, the Kaiser is supposed to have come to Rodin's studio incognito to discuss the possibility of a portrait, reportedly feeling that this gesture would indicate his good will toward the French by honoring their greatest artist. Embarrassed and annoyed, Rodin refused, claiming that he lacked the time. He was occasionally criticized for not doing a portrait of an important public figure. Guillaume Apollinaire noted in his journal Rodin's reply to a query as to why he did not honor Anatole France, who had at one time written favorably on his work: "You know what your Anatole France is? He is just the sauce, without the rabbit." Asked in turn why he did not have the sculptor make a portrait of him, France retorted: "Obviously, your Rodin is a genius, but what of it? To my mind, he is too great a collaborator with catastrophe."[21]

Rodin's most brilliant portrait of a statesman emerged from a series of studies of the head of Georges Clemenceau done in 1911. Clemenceau is supposed to have denounced them all, and did in fact insist that one of the series intended for exhibition at the Salon be titled *Bust of an Unknown*. Later, however, he ad-

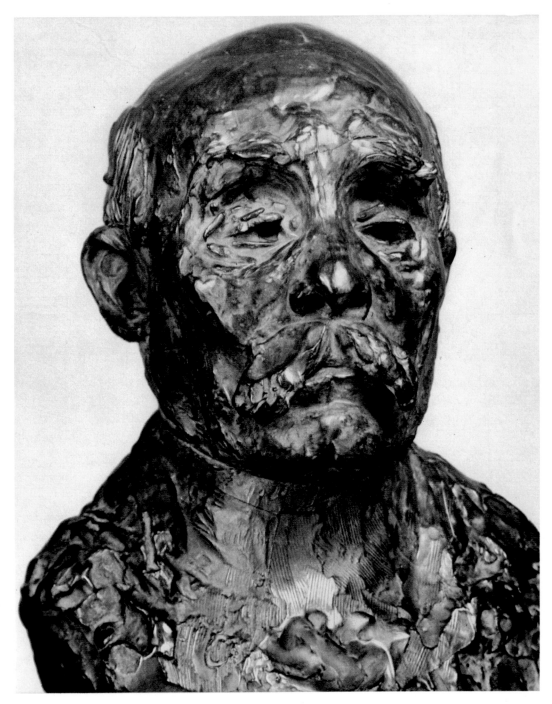

Georges Benjamin Clemenceau. 1911. Bronze, 19″ high

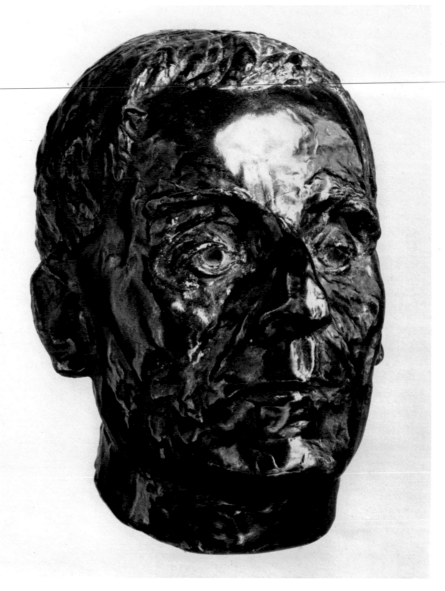

Pope Benedict XV. 1915. Bronze, 10¼″ high

mitted that he did not dislike them all. During the eighteen sittings endured by the fiery, impatient "Tiger," as Clemenceau was nicknamed, Rodin worked for a definitive resemblance, making innumerable notations of the features and researching into each detail of the face. In the best of the series, the sculptor merged the enigmatic mandarin mask, the sarcastic disdain, the obstinacy and the ramrod pride of Clemenceau. The analogy that pleased the artist best was between the portrait and a clenched fist.

When Rodin did not exhibit his latest work immediately in the Salons, the press heaped criticism and charges of cowardice upon him. During the twenty years before his death, the cry was constantly raised that he could not finish anything. To a friend he confided after a year's work on the *Clemenceau*:

> I am still too close to him. I am not sufficiently detached from it to judge or to see it. I must forget what I have done to understand it better. I never consider anything that leaves my hands as completed. I have a complete image of my model. He gave me eighteen sittings. Between times I dreamed of his face, of his expression and of his character. [22]

One of Rodin's last portraits, left incomplete, was of Pope Benedict XV, who impatiently could not comprehend why he had to be studied from all angles. When the sculptor looked down on him, this in effect violated protocol by placing the Pope in an inferior position. [23] Each time that Rodin moved to study a profile, the Pope turned his head to see what was happening. Although only four sittings were permitted, Rodin came away with his most private image of a public figure. The hard traces of the subject's humanity replaced all awareness of his status; in spite of the selfconscious rigidity of the pose and the masklike set of the face, the evidence of the flesh could not be concealed. The result is a head that is powerful in its confrontation of the forces of life and death.

1. *On Art and Artists*, p. 137.
2. *Ibid.*, pp. 145-46.
3. *Ibid.*, p. 65.
4. *Loc. cit.*
5. This analysis is found in the chapter "Of Yesterday and Today," *On Art and Artists*, pp. 137 ff.
6. *Ibid.*, p. 143, p. 156.
7. Père Eymard emerges as anything but a saint from his contact with Rodin; he failed to reimburse the artist for the copies made of the bust (see Biographical Outline, page 205) and complained that Rodin had treated his hair so that he appeared to have horns (Bartlett, *op. cit.*, p. 28).
8. *Loc. cit.* The head also appears in the small terra-cotta version of *The Earth*.
9. *On Art and Artists*, p. 182.
10. Frisch and Shipley, *op. cit.*, pp. 359-60.
11. Grappe (*op. cit.*, p. 87) dates the enlarged head 1890-91.
12. Lawton, *op. cit.*, pp. 163-64.

13. *On Art and Artists*, p. 150.
14. *Ibid.*, p. 156.
15. *Ibid.*, p. 153.
16. Bartlett, *op. cit.*, p. 144.
17. From an article of 1892 in the Musée Rodin's file on the *Baudelaire*; the name of the newspaper is lacking.
18. *Dépêche de Toulouse*, August 21, 1936.
19. *Annales Politiques Littéraires* (Paris), December 2, 1932. In this article, Shaw pointed out that Rodin wanted to show man eternally changing. He also wrote that the sculptor collected stones, especially minerals with strange markings in which he saw people, and that these objects were so numerous that he needed a separate house in which to store them.
20. *Dépêche de Toulouse*, loc. cit.
21. G. Apollinaire, *Chroniques d'Art, 1902-1918*, Paris, Gallimard, 1960, p. 437.
22. Domergue in *Liberté* (Paris), October 10, 1911.
23. Cladel, *Rodin*, p. 251.

The Danaïd. 1885. Marble, 13¾" high × 28½" long × 22¼" deep

THE SCULPTURES IN MARBLE

ALTHOUGH RODIN today is most admired for his bronzes, from 1900 on his preferred material was marble, and more new conceptions emerged from his studio in stone than in bronze. In some respects, the connoisseurship of his marbles is more demanding than that of his bronzes, owing to the varied skills and specializations of his assistants and uncertainty over the extent of the artist's own participation.

One of the strongest criticisms directed against Rodin by the younger generation of sculptors who came to prominence late in his lifetime was that he did not do his own carving in stone and therefore had no true feeling for the medium. They argued that his conceptions were those of a modeler rather than of a carver. It was customary in Rodin's time – and for centuries before – for an artist to work first in clay and plaster before having his conception translated into stone. The advocates of direct carving without recourse to preliminary studies in other mediums might also have condemned Bernini and Michelangelo on the same grounds, since Rodin was actually continuing their tradition. He employed a small group of "practitioners" as the stonecutters who duplicated an artist's work were called.[1] It has often been claimed that Rodin himself never worked in stone and had no training in this medium, but there is evidence to contradict both assertions.

It is true that many of his sculptures in stone were not touched by Rodin, who relied upon assistants such as Bourdelle to interpret faithfully his original plaster model. In his early years, in spite of continued poverty, he seems always to have sought a stone carver to translate his work, beginning with the marble head of *The Man with the Broken Nose* in 1872. There is evidence, however, to suggest that he was trained and experienced in stone carving, and that on occasion he did the fine chiseling and polishing. During the 1870s, when he was serving as a decorator in Belgium, he appears to have actually done some carving in stone, both from his own models and those of his associate, van Rasbourgh.[2] p. 207 For certain of his sculptures, Rodin not only supervised his assistants but also intervened in the cutting. His expertness in finishing his work in stone is suggested by the account of a friend, the sculptor Baffier, whom he invited to do some carving on a sculpture of Victor Hugo. Baffier commented that, after he completed his task, although Rodin did not criticize the clumsiness of his efforts, it meant more work and recutting by the master himself.[3] Judith Cladel recalls that when supervising an assistant's work, he would mark with a pencil the contours to be preserved, the holes to be deepened, and the passages that required more modeling to capture the light. In the early '90s, the writer Remy de Gourmont tells us, Rodin had the work in marble constantly under his eyes.[4]

133

That this was not always the case after 1900 is shown by Mme Bourdelle's recollection of Rodin's arrival at her husband's studio with a small plaster model. After indicating the size he wanted and a few other details, he would depart and not return until the work was near completion or actually finished. On one occasion, Mme Bourdelle remembers that her husband pointed out to Rodin the rough handling of the plaster in a woman's leg and asked if this was to be reproduced literally. Rodin replied in effect that it should not; while it was permissible in plaster, Bourdelle should get a good model and "finish it" in stone.[5] This anecdote serves as a reminder that Rodin did not have the same esthetic for

p. 63

work in different media, as a juxtaposition of the bronze version of *The Kiss* with the marble one instantly reveals. A more feminine or cosmetically attractive mode and idealization of the figure frequently prevailed in stone, which did not tolerate the rugged or ragged passages and the tonal range of shadows found in bronze. To apprehend fully what Rodin sought in stone, the work must be subtly lighted, usually from the side, in order to reveal the multiple, close inflections of a brow or cheek. He could never bring himself to cut into marble the flagrant creases, ridges, pits and crests that scar the bronzes and enrich their surfaces. His eloquent writing about the *Venus de Milo* and his observations about antique marbles seen by candlelight are instructive both as to Rodin's inspiration and his intent. Even in his last days, the translucency and luminosity of fine marble, its susceptibility to almost imperceptible nuances of smoothness, the ambivalent potentialities of its surface for both firmness and liquidity, continued to excite him. In the period after the *Monument to Balzac,* he employed marble more than bronze to simulate flesh and to epitomize the voluptuousness and timeless equanimity he often sought to rival in Greek art.

Young women were the subjects that Rodin interpreted most successfully in marble. Although Maillol criticized Rodin for having copied the wrinkles in an

p. 64
p. 137

old woman's belly, it should be remembered that *The Helmet-Maker's Wife* was rendered in bronze, not in marble. Rodin's *Beside the Sea*, on the other hand, is distinguished by qualities that both Maillol and his admirers have pointed out is common to the work of the two artists. The subject is one of passivity and quiet contemplation. The woman's form reveals itself fully without the need of dramatic lighting. The seated woman is compressed within a roughly cubical form through the drawn-up position of her knees. (The legs have proportions like those found in Maillol's work.) Rodin could not abide complete self-containment, however, and both the woman's left arm and her gaze are turned outward. The illusionistic base upon which she sits was a device not used by Maillol.

Rodin's marbles constitute an Augustan phase of his life, a kind of sweet *détente* in his style. They were suitable for exhibiting either in museums, private homes or gardens. The subjects are generally unproblematic, the esthetic somewhat anodyne. These works coincide with the decline of Rodin's insurgency as social observer and monument maker. He sought what he felt was the artistic

134

The Muse. After 1900. Marble, 19¼″ high × 23⅛″ wide × 17½″ deep

truth known to the Greeks, which arose not from pathetic, strenuous postures but from untroubled, sensitively modeled surfaces:

> If I say that a sculptor can confine himself to representing palpitating flesh, without preoccupying himself with subject, this does not mean that I exclude thought from his work; if I desire that he need not seek symbols, this does not signify that I am a partisan of an art deprived of spiritual significance.... The body always expresses the spirit whose envelope it is. And for him who can see, the nude offers the richest meaning. [6]

Rodin's late marble mode was an art of old age. It issued from the calm that was necessary for the sedentary contemplation of quiet beauty, a calm that he desired after the violence of the years leading up to 1900, and after his own militancy had been largely spent. There is a ludic quality in the making of a personal, floating world of sinless nymphs, zephyrs, satyrs and bathers. Bodies are generally freed of anguish, and frequently of gravity. When sorrow or melan-

Psyche. 1886. Marble, 24″ high

Beside the Sea. 1905. Marble, 23½″ high × 35″ long × 22⅞″ deep

p. 132 choly appears, as in *The Danaïd*, it is bittersweet, not barbed or body-wracking. Water sprites and satyrs replace the morbid populace of *The Gates of Hell*, and Rodin's youthful commitment to the ancient dionysiac world seen *à travers* eighteenth-century art floats again to the top of his artistic consciousness. He found in antiquity an uninhibited world of playful amorous feeling that bore out his view that "love is essentially copulation. The rest is only detail, doubtless charming, but detail nevertheless."[7]

The flowing quality of flesh, hair and wings in these works is never stylized in the manner of Art Nouveau. To the end of his life, Rodin resisted the idea of consciously imposing a style on his subjects. Those sculptors obsessed with the need for "style" and "the architectural" in sculpture, such as Bourdelle, were often dismayed at Rodin's frank illusionism and self-effacement before the model. He never honored the shape of the original block of stone to an extent that would allow the imagination to reconstruct it from the final carving. Be-p. 136 ginning about 1886, in his *Psyche*, however, he does seem to have preserved references to the stages by which the stone was metamorphosed from its primal opaque, obdurate, quarried state into flesh.[8] This mingling of the complete with the incomplete unquestionably came initially from Rodin's contact with Michelangelo rather than from Carrière, with whose painting this device has affinities. Rodin once explained this aspect of his style as follows:

> No good sculptor can model a human figure without dwelling on the mystery of life; this individual and that in fleeting variations only reminds him of the immanent type; he is led perpetually from the creature to the creator.... All the best works of any artist must be bathed, so to speak, in mystery. That is why many of my figures have a hand, a foot still imprisoned in the marble block; life is everywhere, but rarely indeed does it come to complete expression or the individual to perfect freedom.[9]

Rodin was too much of an illusionist–or naturalist, as he preferred to be called– to flatten surfaces, compress limbs or circumscribe long, flowing hair in order to give his marble a tidy, concentric blockiness. The stone might suggest to him (as it did to Bernini, whom he particularly admired on a trip to Rome in 1912) clouds, vapors, caves, waves, some palpable environment by which he might enhance the mystery or charm of a figure.

Rodin's works in marble do not today ignite the imagination nor challenge the eye as do his bronzes, which in individual, climactic and brilliant works show more frequently and spectacularly the unflinching concentration of his gifts. But the better marbles, such as the women's portraits, *The Danaïd* and *Beside the Sea,* are generally suffused with good taste. Frequently they will reveal superb passages of finesse in modeling that compensate for the triviality and lack of inspiration in many of his other marbles. For better or worse, Rodin's marble mode was one that came honestly and naturally to him; and even when we are not in sympathy with his song, we can always enjoy his voice.

1. Rodin had several assistants throughout his career. Besides Antoine Bourdelle and Jules Desbois, who did a considerable amount of work in stone for him, other assistants included the Schnegg brothers, Charles Despiau, Dejean Drivier, François Pompon, Alexandre Charpentier, Victor Frisch, Jean Halou, Jean Escoula, the Czech Josef Maratka, the Russian Soudbinine and the Swiss Rodo de Nederhäusern.

2. L. Bénédite, *Rodin*, Paris, 1926, p. 10.

3. Lawton, *op. cit.*, p. 64. He adds: "The touching up with the chisel, of course, Rodin always reserved for himself in its ultimate and finest execution."

4. Remy de Gourmont, "Le Marbre et la chair," *Journal* (Paris), November 11, 1893.

5. Interview of the author with Mme Bourdelle, July 11, 1962.

6. *On Art and Artists*, pp. 176–77.

7. Cladel, *Rodin, l'homme et l'oeuvre*, p. 56.

8. Grappe, *op. cit.*, p. 55, *s. v.* "Psyche."

9. Harris, *loc. cit.*

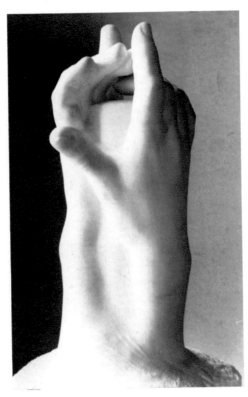

The Secret. 1910. Marble, 35″ high

Three Male Studies.

Left: *Seated Man, Legs Extended.* Terra cotta, 6¼″ high

Below: left, *Crouching Man.* Terra cotta, 5¼″ high

Below: *Seated Man: Study for "The Thinker."* Terra cotta, 9⅜″ high

RODIN'S IMPROVISATIONS

RODIN'S SMALL SCULPTURES, which were not the result of commissions but were of a purely private nature, came to the attention of artists and collectors during the late 1940s and '50s, largely through the exhibitions held by the late Curt Valentin at his gallery in New York. These acrobats, dancers and bathers were modeled in clay and for the most part were cast in bronze only after the sculptor's death. In the basement of Rodin's former studio at the Villa des Brillants, Meudon (administered by the Musée Rodin in Paris, and restored partly through the generosity of the late Jules E. Mastbaum of Philadelphia), there are hundreds of these small sculptures. Some are still unidentified, many uncast, unphotographed and unpublished, and mostly inaccessible to the general public. A veritable *Rodin inconnu* exists today in the Meudon basement, and this title, in fact, was recently given to an exhibition of the artist's works held at the Louvre, which included a number of these figures along with many from the Musée Rodin in Paris and from other public and private collections.[1]

These sculptures, which Rodin called his "snakes," were the result of serious play and improvisation.[2] They were not always made directly from the model. Even when conversing with visitors, the artist obsessively worked the clay, forming it into torsos often smaller than his hands. He would make quick clay sketches for friends to demonstrate his knowledge of the structure of the figure in different periods of art history. Often while his models were walking about the studio, Rodin made impressions of their movements without removing his eyes from their bodies.[3] On one occasion, Mme Rodin in a violent rage charged into the studio, ordinarily forbidden to her, and chased her husband around the room. Rodin continued modeling Rose's face without looking at the clay and, at the end of the chase, remarked: "Thank you, my dear. That was excellent."[4]

Never one to wait for inspiration, Rodin made a constant practice of working in the studio nearly every day. This helps to explain his tremendous productivity. He believed that the true qualities of an artist were wisdom, attentiveness, sincerity and will–all the virtues of the "honest worker."

Consistency was not one of his virtues. It seems odd to read from the man who had made *The Burghers of Calais*: "One must never try to express an idea by form. Make your form, make something, and the idea will come."[5] On another occasion, he gave this most revealing description of his creative process:

> I often begin with one intention and finish with another. While fashioning my clay, I see in fancy something that had been lying dormant in my memory and which rises up before me in what seems to be a vision created by myself. I know it is not this, but a suggested combination of form which I must have already

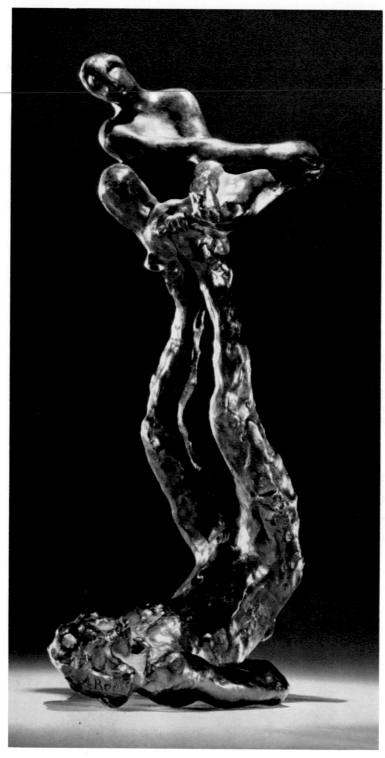

The Juggler. 1892–95. Bronze, 11¼″ high

142

Nijinsky. 1912. Bronze, 6¾″ high

perceived in nature, and which has never before aroused in me the image that corresponds to it. And then, as I go on, and the execution becomes more complete, there is a sort of reverse process in my mind, and that which I have made reacts on my perception of nature, and I find resemblances and fresh analogies which fill me with joy.[6]

The finished forms suggested their titles: "The title depends upon what strikes you first, or most strongly. Always the forms give rise to the ideas."[7] If there is a parallel between Rodin's art and that of late nineteenth-century painters such p. 142 as Toulouse-Lautrec, it can be seen in such works as *The Juggler*, in which it is the form rather than the subject which first reveals itself to the beholder. In the life-size sculptures, most of which were enlargements of small studies, Rodin p. 54 was still committed to a type of faithful anatomical rendering, as in *The Thinker*. It is his small, improvised works that are the most emancipated from references either to anatomy or to earlier prototypes in art and are the most revealing of decisions made during the work process. Modeling on a less strenuous scale, with the play of wrist and fingers unimpeded, the sculptor could respond without reflection to the life of fancy and instinct that lay in his fingertips. A superb craftsman, possessed of marvelous dexterity and endless tricks by which he could instantaneously and succinctly transpose into clay his most elusive ideas or

Bather. c. 1900. Terra cotta, 19¾" high.

feelings, Rodin trusted his eyes as the final arbiters of esthetic rightness. Although his surfaces, which were the essence of his art, became less literal anatomically, they are never abstract or without rough correspondence to the human body. However cursory or contorted, the "snakes" are always plausible.

In pieces such as the small *Nijinsky* of 1912, the mass of the body has been *p. 143* violently broken into, rendered almost molten, a composite of the energies the dancer displayed during a private performance for Rodin. The limits of the gestures are roughly established, while the constant understanding of details, including the silhouette, contributes to an immediacy of all-over effect that is achieved with far less effort than in a large sculpture, the *Balzac* for instance. *p. 88* The raw traces left by the activity of the artist's fingers make this *Nijinsky* sketch an intimate revelation, establishing a bond between artist and viewer that is difficult to attain in the more formal public images. The creative process apparent in these sculptural sketches is an essential component of their expressiveness.

Rodin's improvisations also show his disinclination toward the concept of "style" which emerged in the 1880s as a conscious imposition of the artist's personality on his subject through distortion or stylization. Rodin was unable to predetermine his style before encountering his model; in his own words: "He who sells himself to a style turns his statues into bad literature."[8]

What now seems heroic and contemporary about Rodin is not only his vision of the pathetic victim-hero who reacts rather than acts, nor his struggle to portray the emotional and psychological complexity of living human beings, but his passion for the act of *making* rather than *completing* sculpture. During his creative moments, the best of the artist found its outlet through his fingertips. His personal problem was in setting for himself impossible absolutes of perfection toward which he dedicated a lifetime of striving. It is doubtful that at his death he would have pronounced any of his works finished or immutable.

RODIN AND DEGAS

The artist whose sculpture is closest to Rodin's in the study of movement is Degas. The two men were good friends and had mutual respect for each other's work. Degas was a frequent visitor to Meudon, and presumably Rodin was one of the few permitted to see Degas' sculpture, which (with one exception) was neither cast nor exhibited during his lifetime. When Rodin asked Degas why he was unwilling to cast his work in bronze, the latter replied: "It's too great a responsibility. Bronze is for eternity. You know how I like to work these figures over and over. When one crumbles, I have an excuse for beginning again."[9]

There is no specific evidence of an exchange of influence between the two artists, and since almost all Degas' sculptures are undated, it is difficult to compare their work year by year. Comparison of their art helps, however, to make clear both the interests they shared and the deep differences that perhaps precluded

Edgar Degas. *Dancers*. Bronze. Left to right:
Fourth Position Front, on the Left Leg, 22⅝″ high;
Fourth Position Front, on the Left Leg, 22⅜″ high;
Grande Arabesque, Third Time, 17¼″ high

Three Dance Movements. 1911. Bronze.
Left to right: *Dance Movement C,* 13⅞″ high;
Dance Movement B, 12¾″ high;
Dance Movement A, 12¼″ high

one from influencing the other. Degas' sculptures came naturally from his pre-occupations in painting. Like Rodin, he refused to allow his models to take the conventional Salon poses; for his sculpture as for his painting, he drew upon his contacts with life outside of the art schools and museums. He, like Rodin, was absorbed with natural movements that were wholly unrelated to rhetorical or heroic expression, but his sculptures of women represented the movements of *daily life*, while Rodin called in circus performers, cancan dancers or vaudeville acrobats to pose in the nude for him. Rodin generally sought from his models unpremeditated, impulsive, spontaneous and unusual movements, while Degas firmly fixed his models in poses and generally preferred these to be the trained, habitual postures and gestures that were part of the woman's everyday routine. Rodin's models were encouraged to move freely, giving uninhibited expression to every whim or emotion, as in the modern dance. (He greatly admired Loïe Fuller and Isadora Duncan.) The models who served Degas assumed poses

p. 147

Edgar Degas. *Woman Putting on Her Stocking.*
Bronze, 17″ high

Dance Movement D. 1911. Bronze, 13″ high

Study. Female Torso. c. 1900. Plaster

dictated either by their professional training, such as the classical ballet, or that *p. 146* had become automatic through such daily rituals as washing, drying of the hair or body, fastening or unfastening clothes, or stretching fatigued backs and muscles after working. Degas presented a disenchanted view of women circumscribed by a routinized existence that allowed for no display of character and emotion. Rodin's sculpture showed the emancipated, passionate woman whose body was exquisitely attuned to every nuance of feeling.

These differences may be accounted for by the divergent temperaments and sexual natures of the two sculptors. Rodin's unconcealed and endless lust and his numerous liaisons are as well known as his sculpture. After 1900 it became fashionable for society women, who had paid the fee of forty thousand francs to sit for their portraits, to write in their memoirs or insinuate privately that Rodin had at least suggested an affair. In his sculpture, women are the eternal objects of desire; no matter how fragmentary or coarse the execution, his art is that of the body loved. Never in Degas' work do we see a frank exposure of the sexual organs as in Rodin's *Study: Female Torso* or *Iris, Messenger of the Gods* (which was *p. 185* known for a time as *The Eternal Tunnel*). Degas' women are neither sensual nor sexual. His relation to his models was described by Victor Frisch, who as Rodin's assistant after 1890 knew the studio talk:

> Degas, unlike Rodin, had the reputation of using his models only to paint. He had no weakness for women, it is said. On the contrary, he longed for them deeply; but alas, yearned not merely to possess them, but to possess the initial courage to reach out to them. He was prey to an adolescent shyness, a fear of refusal, a preliminary embarrassment and shame, that kept him from moving along the amorous way. His tentative questing, with his models, would be checked, then turned as a jesting; so that Degas grew to be known not as a lover but as a prankster, and all the practical jokes of the bohemian quarter were attributed to him. [10]

Beautiful as Degas' female figures are as sculpture, they leave one with a sense of disenchantment because they lack sensuously modeled body surfaces. Rodin could never suppress his commitment to reproducing not only the seductiveness of flesh but also the bodily grace that was admired by the Greeks and the artists of the Renaissance. Degas' girl bathing, in *The Tub*, is all elbows and ankles, re- *p. 152* duced to the awkwardness of an animal by the act of washing herself. Rodin's women are often rendered as animals, but with a feral grace and passion that enhance their femininity.

In some ways, Degas was more daring than Rodin, notably in his literal as well as figurative removal of woman from her pedestal. We must look down to his *Tub*, which rests directly on the floor at our feet, for the sculpture has been modeled from this standpoint. The closest that Rodin may have come to eliminating the base was in exhibiting his bronze *Eve* in 1898, when the stand was *p. 51* buried in the sand of the exhibition hall; and perhaps in the recumbent *Martyr*, *p. 153* originally a standing figure in *The Gates of Hell*. Rodin made no adjustments in

p. 147, 149 the position or weight of limbs in this recumbent version and seems to have designed no base for it. His suite of dancers, done after 1900, also lacked bases, and the terra-cotta originals must be artificially supported to be seen upright. When Degas' figures required external supports, it was due to faulty armatures and his ignorance of, and impatience with, mere craftsmanship, for his intent was to p. 146 search for an infinite variety of self-balancing postures. (Like Rodin, he had a great instinct for finding the body's center of gravity.) Rodin's *Spirit of Eternal* p. 154 *Repose*, by contrast, is able to lean against a pillar of air because of the sculptor's marvelous command of armature construction.

The freshness and vigor of Degas' modeling, so much admired today among sculptors, resulted from a more thorough empiricism in discovering and reconstituting the body's mass (he himself complained of his limited knowledge of anatomy); whereas Rodin's method was deeply involved with historical techniques. Once having established the gesture and located the body's mass, Degas often created a surface texture that was more arbitrary than that of Rodin, by flattening touches of clay but refusing to blend them or to represent musculature in a literal fashion. That many of the figures cast in bronze after Degas' death were fragmentary was the result not of intent but of accident, as parts were continually falling off or disintegrating. This accidental segmentation is quite different from the intentional kind found either in his painting or in Rodin's sculpture.

Edgar Degas. *The Tub.* Bronze, 18¼″ high × 16¼″ long

152

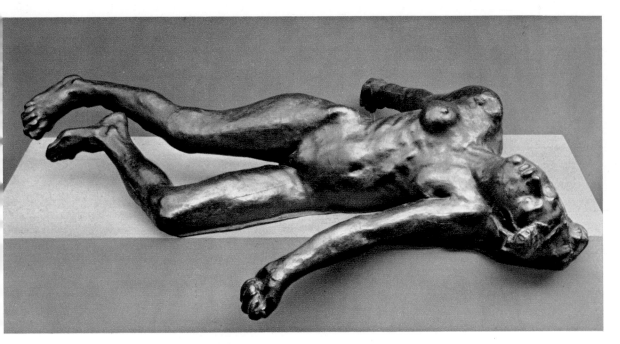

The Martyr. 1884. Bronze, 16⅜″ high × 61⅜″ long

1. Paris, Musée du Louvre, December 1962-January 1963.

2. Frisch and Shipley, *op. cit.*, p. 420.

3. "I am accustomed to having my models wander naked about the studio. They walk or rest.... I familiarize myself with all of their movements. I constantly note the association of their feelings and the line of their bodies, and by this observation I accustom myself to discover the expression of the soul, not only in the features of the face, but in the entire human form. I do not impose any attitude upon them, but when I discover what seems to be a characteristic gesture, I ask them to stop and I immediately begin to make a drawing or a small clay sketch. I have thus made innumerable sketches but it is rare that they serve me as preparatory models for more advanced work.

I never repeat myself. When I feel like modeling a figure of important dimensions, I attack it immediately and carry it to the degree of completion that I judge to be right" ("Rodin raconté par lui-même," *La Revue*, May, 1906).

4. Frisch and Shipley, *op. cit.*, p. 340.

5. *Ibid.*, p. 201.

6. Lawton, *op. cit.*, pp. 162–63.

7. Frisch and Shipley, *op. cit.,* p. 202.

8. *Ibid.*, p. 203.

9. *Ibid.*, p. 312.

10. *Ibid.*, p. 316. One of the most amusing of Degas' pranks recounted by Frisch was that in which he told a certain young model that she had "the pear-shaped buttocks of the *Mona Lisa.*" The gullible girl went about the studios, hopefully making this recommendation known to prospective employers.

The Spirit of Eternal Repose. 1899.
Plaster, 76¾" high

Nude with Drapery. Pencil and watercolor, 17½″ × 12½″. The Art Institute of Chicago
(The Alfred Stieglitz Collection)

RODIN'S DRAWINGS

p. 38

THE BASIS of Rodin's art was drawing from nature – and "nature" to him meant the naked human body. Except for the architectural sketches he made on visits to the Gothic cathedrals, or as studies for *The Gates of Hell*, most of his thousands of sketches were of the living model, either observed or remembered. The sketches that appeared in *Les Cathédrales de France*, reproducing studies made on the spot over many years, are not architect's renderings but revelations of a sculptor's interest in the physiognomy of each building, its distinctive gestures, rhythms and shadows. Rodin felt the thrust and hollow of a portal were analogous to the saliences and depressions of a body's surface.

During the late 1870s and early '80s, Rodin experienced a fantasist phase, in which feelings and visions dominated perception, resulting in some of his most interesting drawings.[1] Significantly, they were inspired by literature such as Dante's *Inferno* and included obsessive themes in which passion is enacted more strongly than anywhere else in his art. Images of rape, murder and self-destruction intermingle with the haunting apparition of the horse and rider, and the amorous coupling of women with the devil. Many of these drawings have in common a heavy penumbra of ink and gouache that corrodes or stops out the linear silhouettes. By the early 1880s, however, when in making *The Gates of Hell* Rodin confronted the questions of reality and relevance to his time, he seems to have turned against his own spirit of fantasy that had found expression in these drawings. Thereafter, his sculpture and his drawings were increasingly made from life.

p. 36
p. 156

The wealth of meaning and personal revelation that are contained in the little-known and largely unstudied drawings of around 1880 can be seen in the series of studies showing a type of naked male dance, which culminated in the drypoint and etching, *La Ronde*, made by Rodin in 1883.[2] The subject is the curious enactment of a dance that seems compulsive, rather than ritualistic or spontaneously joyful, and is accompanied by solemn watchers in an austere setting. The principal source was probably Canto XVI of the *Inferno*, in which Dante and Virgil encounter the homosexuals, whose punishment for "violence against nature" was perpetual movement beneath an eternal rain of burning sand. When confronted by Dante, some of the damned "made of themselves a wheel." They are described as athletic and naked, moving in an unco-ordinated fashion, "so that the neck kept traveling in a direction contrary to the feet."[3] *La Ronde*, meaning each in his turn, suggests that Rodin was evolving a personal interpretation of the Wheel of Fortune as a commentary on human destiny. The pervasiveness of the wheel, both as form and morbid symbol, can be seen in *The Gates of Hell*, where it is actually held in the hand of an angel who lies

p. 157

p. 34

Horseman. 1889. Gouache, pen and ink. 8¼″ × 6⅞″.
The Art Institute of Chicago (The Alfred Stieglitz Collection)

Satan Embracing a Woman ("L'Avenir"). c. 1880.
Gouache, pen and ink. Whereabouts unknown

p. 84, 85 above the left tomb, and in the later *ronde*-like composition of *The Burghers of Calais*, whose figures were originally modeled nude, in postures that recall the dance. Rodin's print of *La Ronde*, exhibited in 1905, may have been seen by Matisse before he inserted the dancers in his composition of the *Joie de Vivre*. But while Matisse showed dancing women as emancipated spirits, made light of foot by their freedom of feeling, Rodin portrayed men whose tread is burdened by guilt for their passionate crimes. Possibly the *Joie de Vivre* was Matisse's partial answer to Rodin's earlier pessimism about the passions and the dominance of emotion over reason.

Rarely did Rodin make a sculpture from his own drawings. On the other hand, he made many sketches from his own sculptures—for example, one prob-
p. 158 ably drawn from a work of the 1870s entitled *Springtime*, and later others from
p. 24 *The Age of Bronze, St. John the Baptist Preaching* and the *Monument to Balzac*, to name but a few. The habit of drawing from sculpture may have resulted from his youthful training in sketching from casts of antique sculpture and served

La Ronde. 1883. Etching and drypoint, 3¾″ × 5⅝″

Study for "La Ronde". Pencil, 3 × 3½″.
Collection Mrs. Jane Wade Lombard, New York

him as a private analysis of modeling. Drawings he made after the Medici Tombs aided his search for the principles Michelangelo had used in constructing and animating his figures and helped Rodin to understand how these differed from his own work.[4]

Drawing enabled Rodin to understand art as well as nature, and on a few occasions it served directly for self-study. There are two known self-portrait drawings, one of 1859 and the other of approximately the late 1870s[5] (still others may exist in the private archives of the Musée Rodin). In the earlier of these Rodin, with a curious kind of delicacy, showed himself as a handsome young man. The later one is a darker, tenser rendering, with a preponderance of

Springtime. Pencil, 17¼″ × 11¼″.
Collection Mr. and Mrs. Hugo Perls, New York

Drawing after Michelangelo's "Day." Charcoal, 16½ × 23½". Musée Rodin, Paris

shadow, contracted brows, and an over-all forceful intensity compressed within a blocky silhouette. More revealing than a photograph, it provides us with a provocative self-image of the artist on the eve of the creation of *The Gates of Hell*.

To sketch in pencil was as natural and habitual with Rodin as was modeling. Drawing always remained for him a means by which he could prepare, test and preserve the immediate co-ordination between eye and hand that was required for the perfect rendition of emotion when transposing life into art: "No sudden inspiration can replace the long toil which is indispensable to give the eye a true knowledge of form and of proportion and to render the hand obedient to the commands of feeling."[6]

Drawing, however, was always subservient to sculpture in Rodin's eyes. His brilliance as a draftsman had been recognized early, as is evidenced by the prizes he won at the Petite Ecole before he was seventeen and by his acceptance as a drawing student at the Ecole des Beaux-Arts at the age of eighteen. But Rodin would not enter the School on the basis of his drawing, believing that his talent and future lay in sculpture, even though he failed the entrance examinations for this on three occasions. Only rarely did he exhibit his drawings, and then in conjunction with his sculpture, as in the great retrospective at the Paris Exposition Universelle in 1900. A notable exception was the extensive showing of his drawings at Stieglitz's "291" Gallery in New York in 1908 – an exhibition made possible by the friendship between the artist and Edward Steichen. In speaking to others, Rodin often deprecated his drawings as merely personal *études*, not finished work.

Yet it is evident that he not only saw his drawing in terms of sculpture, but his modeling in terms of drawing. Both depended upon observation of the edges that the figure presented. A common test for the success of either drawn or modeled edge was the absence of dry, inert passages. He frequently referred to the silhouettes of his busts as "lines," while describing his drawings in terms of "profiles." As already noted, in the *Balzac* he sought "the great lines" so that he might avoid obscuring the strength of his design by details. He used both media for uninhibited explorations of movement, frank studies of the private parts of the naked female body, or such themes as Lesbian lovemaking. How closely Rodin felt toward his drawings is illustrated by those instances in which, desiring to make a gift to a friend, he would present him with a copy of the original, while retaining the latter in his private folios.

Rodin derived both his belief in the importance of drawing from nature and his technique as draftsman from one of the nineteenth century's most gifted teachers, unfortunately little known today, by whom he had the good fortune to be trained from the ages of fourteen through seventeen. In a letter of appreciation to the publisher of Horace Lecoq de Boisbaudran's *L'Education de la mémoire pittoresque et la formation de l'artiste*, Rodin wrote in 1913: "The greatest part of what he taught remains with me still."[7] Since the 1840s, Rodin's teacher at the Petite Ecole had developed a highly personal, systematic, but for that time unorthodox method of enriching his students' memories and imaginations, while insuring their integrity and individuality as artists. To Lecoq de Boisbaudran, memory meant the preservation of direct observation; it was his task to impart to his students the means that would enable them to respond to future inspiration.

Essentially, his method consisted in gradually removing the model, after having given his students time to develop their own devices for fixing its characteristics in their memories. He suggested these devices, but did not impose them. For students of Rodin's age, study of the body began with single features, such as the nose, mouth, or eyes, before starting on heads–at first simple, then complex. Students were never allowed to look at one another's work, nor at their master's. To stimulate the process of conjuring up the absent image in their minds, Lecoq de Boisbaudran had them memorize traditional precepts of attention to size, gesture, value and color. One part of the model's body served as a module for the dimensions. Salient movements were established by intersecting vertical and horizontal lines, or by framing the figure within a box in order to measure more precisely the position of the limbs. (Perhaps it was as a result of this training that Rodin was later to speak of using an invisible cube as his guide in making such figures as those for *The Burghers of Calais*.) The range of values was established by selecting the lightest and darkest areas; similarly, modeling depended upon finding the deepest recessions and most salient projections. At the outset, strict resemblance was the goal, the necessary preface to "interpretation" that would come later with maturity. Thirteen studies by the young Rodin in the Musée Rodin apparently reflect this phase of Lecoq de Boisbaudran's training. The teacher's constant injunction to his pupils, later to be incessantly echoed by Rodin, was: "The true object of study is nature. He who takes his style from this master will attain the greatest originality."[8]

As an antidote to classroom monotony, and to the rigidity of the model on a high stand and his weariness and loss of expression after hours of posing, Rodin's teacher took his students outdoors into the woods, to draw from clothed and nude models who were allowed to move at will. (This was undoubtedly the source of Rodin's later practice of having his models wander freely about the studio.) He also encouraged his charges to draw while walking in the streets. Rodin's adherence to his teacher's advice is illustrated by a notebook, formerly in the collection of Jules E. Mastbaum, and probably dating from the late '50s; besides copies of paintings, it contains sketches of horses, bathers in a public bath house, and a horse and carriage plunging down the street. To assist the

Two Sheets from a Sketchbook. Left: *Bathers*. Ink. Formerly Jules E. Mastbaum Collection. Right: *Two Standing Male Nudes*. Pencil, pen and ink, 7⅜″ × 4⅛″. Jules E. Mastbaum Collection (Courtesy Mrs. Jefferson Dickson, New York)

student in making drawings from life outside the studio, Lecoq de Boisbaudran suggested tracing the outlines of the subject in the air with a finger or drawing point, then repeating this with eyes closed to fix the image in the mind. This aided the young artist in his quest for the great lines of the mass, through simplifying the ensemble before attempting to re-create its details. Similarly, shadows were also omitted at the outset so that everything might be subordinated to the mass.

Before encouraging his students to give their hands and imaginations free play, Lecoq de Boisbaudran drilled them first in working from the model and in prolonged, minute study of anatomy and physiology. He believed that the artist could capture freedom of movement and lifelike action only by the most arduous discipline. He set up classroom exercises that involved drawing a moving figure, first exaggerating all projections that its bones would make (in other words, a living skeleton), and then indicating the outlines of all the muscles and their ligaments with the bones (thereby creating a living écorché). Some of Rodin's drawings of the 1870s, perhaps inspired by Dante and not done directly from the model, show this latter type of muscular reconstruction of male figures in motion.

Lecoq de Boisbaudran did not use the system he had originated as a substitute for the traditional discipline of work from antique casts. (Bartlett mentions that during the 1860s Rodin had plaster casts, including one of the *Venus de Milo*, in his studio.) He had scrupulous standards of accuracy and perfection, and Rodin recalled that in spite of the originality of his teaching he observed tradition, and his studio could be said to be in the eighteenth-century manner.[9] Rodin and others, including Alphonse Legros and later Fantin-Latour, were made to copy eighteenth-century engravings with exactitude, which largely accounts for the sculptor's lifelong love for the art of that period. His teacher's tolerance of many sources of beauty, in the belief that the beautiful, the noble and the true, as well as the new, could be found outside of antiquity, was of incalculable importance to Rodin's nascent esthetic. Lecoq de Boisbaudran nevertheless thought that study from the antique developed taste and afforded the artist the means of correcting faults in the model. The general physical health and sound bodily formation of Rodin's sculptured figures may have resulted from this early teaching. Rodin, who lacked formal education at the *lycée*, may also have received from his drawing master the incentive to expose himself to music and literature, and encouragement to cultivate his intellect simultaneously with his memory and technical dexterity.

The history of Rodin's own development in drawing is the justification for this somewhat lengthy digression on his great teacher. It took Rodin a lifetime to fulfil the ideals of Lecoq de Boisbaudran, and there is little in his drawing after the age of seventeen that did not proceed logically from the teaching to which he had been subjected when he may still have been too young to appreciate the scope and importance of what he was learning.

Even after 1900, Rodin was paraphrasing his teacher. Although lacking wash additions, a suite of ink drawings in the collection of Mr. and Mrs. Charles J. Solomon may illustrate this description of his drawing method: *p. 164*

> For my work of modeling I have not only to possess a very complete *knowledge* of the human form, but also a deep *feeling* for every aspect of it. I have, as it were, to *incorporate* the lines of the human body, and they must become part of myself, deeply seated in my instincts. I must become permeated with the secrets of all its contours, all the masses that it presents to the eye. I must feel them at the end of my fingers. All this must flow naturally from my eye to my hand.... Now look! What is this drawing? Not once in describing the shape of that mass did I shift my eyes from the model. Why? Because I wanted to be sure that nothing evaded my grasp of it. Not a thought about the technical problem of representing it on paper could be allowed to arrest the flow of my feelings about it, from my eye to my hand. The moment I drop my eyes that flow stops. That is why my drawings are only my way of testing myself. They are my way of proving to myself how far this incorporation of the subtle secrets of the human form has taken place within me. I try to see the figure as a mass, as volume. It is this voluminousness that I try to understand. This is why... I sometimes wash a tint over my drawings. This completes the impression of massiveness, and helps me to ascertain how far I have succeeded in grasping the movement as a mass.... My object is to test to what extent my hands already feel what my eyes see. [10]

The stylistic development of Rodin's drawings cannot be dated and charted until the several thousand drawings in the Musée Rodin have been published or made available for study. [11] As is the case with his sculpture, changes in the formal characteristics of his drawing during a given period are due to his responsiveness to a particular model rather than to stylization. "No style is good except that which effaces itself in order to concentrate all the attention of the viewer upon the subject treated, upon the emotion rendered." [12]

In the 1880s, the line drawings that accompanied Baudelaire's *Flowers of Evil* *p. 165* show that Rodin had achieved a style in which all modeling and illusion of depth could be omitted. These pure contour drawings–contemporaneous with, but not dependent upon, the emergence of flattened planes in the Synthetist painting of the mid-'80s–locked the figure to the paper's surface. Probably by the 1890s, Rodin introduced flat, transparent and uniform washes that were placed like a veil over and within the silhouetted figures, abetting the suggestion of volume and movement set up by the line. This device can be seen in a drawing of a later date from the Alfred Stieglitz Collection in the Art Institute of *facing p. 155* Chicago that also bears a striking resemblance to Renoir's later sculpture of the *Standing Venus*. The omission of ground lines and settings of any sort served to suspend the figure within the edges of the paper. With the sureness of an Oriental artist, Rodin often disposed the figure eccentrically on the sheet in ways that required no additional buttressing for visual stability.

Drawing gave Rodin a quicker means and more frequent opportunity than

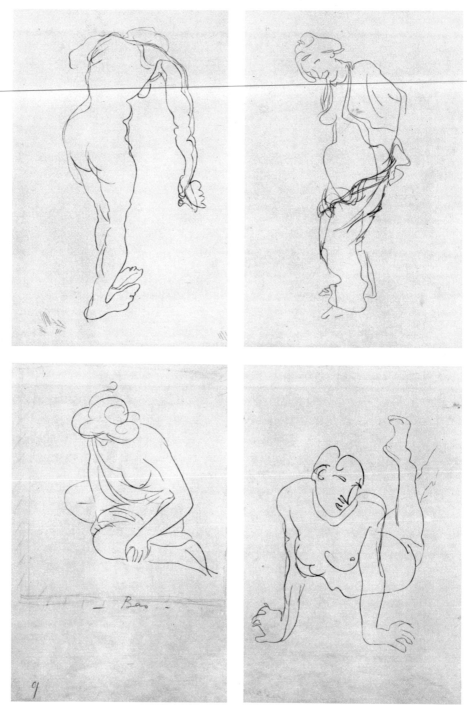

Above, left, *Bending Nude Seen from the Rear*. Ink over pencil, 15⅜" × 10¼"; above, right, *Woman Undressing*. Ink over pencil, 15¼" × 11⅜"; below, left, *Seated Woman*. Ink over pencil, 15¼" × 10⅜"; below, right, *Reclining Nude Resting on Arms*. Ink over pencil, 15⅛" × 11⅜". Collection Mr. and Mrs. Charles J. Solomon, Philadelphia

Drawing for Baudelaire's "L'Imprévu." 1886–88. Ink. Musée Rodin, Paris

modeling by which to enlarge his understanding of movement. The completed sketches, drawn in haste, tumbled from his hands to the floor while his concentration remained riveted on the subject. Later he would flesh out the pencil sketch with a tinted wash. Sketching from dancers required the utmost speed. *p. 166* Some of the purest expressions of the spirit he found in dances ranging from the cancan to the improvisations of Loïe Fuller and Isadora Duncan, the sponta- *p. 168* neous gyrations of an inspired studio model, and Cambodian religious rituals. A wash-and-pencil drawing in the City Art Museum of St. Louis is one of sev- *p. 167* eral that Rodin made while the royal troupe of Cambodian dancers performed during 1906 at his house in Meudon, in Paris and in Marseilles. For all its prescribed nature, their dance presented countless movements new to the artist, who never ceased to be enchanted by the youthful performers. His drawing shows his complete alertness to the importance of the dancer's total gesture. The pointedness of the extremities has been somewhat mitigated, perhaps by Rodin's long habit of rendering the female body sensuously. In contrast to the purity and sureness of the brush movement, the initial pencil drawing, which finally seems superfluous, is more tentative. The wash permitted correcting of proportions and gave greater continuity to the body's mass; but the brush, like

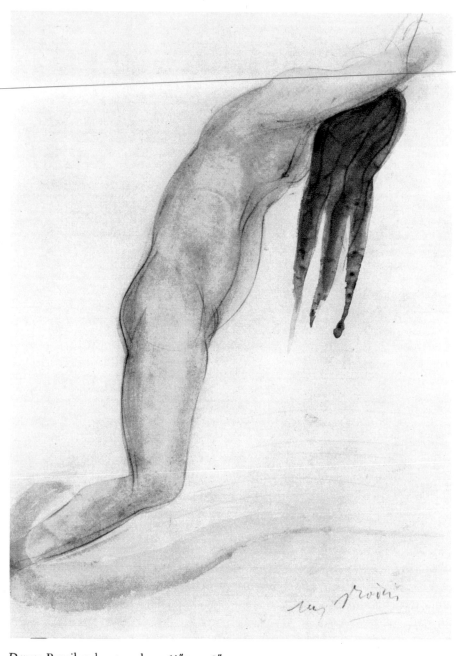

Dancer. Pencil and watercolor, $16\frac{3}{4}'' \times 11\frac{7}{8}''$.
The Museum of Modern Art, New York (Dance and Theater Collection)

the pencil's tip, can still be felt to have followed the contours of the subject. Although the superb balance of these dancers would have allowed them to sustain a pose, there is no evidence that Rodin made sculptures of them.

A drawing in The Art Institute of Chicago shows one of his studio models in the ecstatic abandon of the dance. As with the sculpture of *The Walking Man*, the body is not frozen in a fixed stance; the lines of the figure often begin and end at different moments of its displacement. What is no longer seen – for example, the movement of a sleeve – Rodin indicates summarily with the freest kind of swinging wrist motion. Those who have tried to forge this type of drawing betray themselves by their lack of Rodin's passion, which is revealed in a hundred different ways – by the varied pressures on the drawing point or the impulsive, quick envelopment of a swelling curve or hollow, as if the artist sought to possess the body he drew.

p. 168
p. 28

Cambodian Dancer. 1906. Pencil and watercolor, 16¼″ × 10¾″.
City Art Museum of St. Louis

Woman Dancing. Pencil. 12⅛″ × 7¾″.
The Art Institute of Chicago (The Alfred
Stieglitz Collection)

Study of Isadora Duncan. Pencil and watercolor,
12¼″ × 9″. Collection Mr. and Mrs. Leonard Baskin,
Northampton, Massachusetts

From the 1880s until his death, Rodin moved in the direction of an increased
simplification that enhanced the immediacy of effect in his drawings. Linear inflections might be fewer and seemingly effortlessly achieved; or, as in the draw-

p. 164 ing of a model seen from the rear, there might be the sense of a desperate force.
There were no erasures. Multiple silhouettes of a limb would be retained as part
of the finished fabric, much in the manner of Matisse's drawings and paintings
after 1900. No matter how abbreviated Rodin's notation of an extremity or
how casual his indication of a complex, foreshortened posture, his knowledge of
anatomy was faultless—a fact often overlooked by forgers of his drawings. His
shorthand code for the human form (like that found later in the drawings of
Matisse and Picasso, possibly influenced by his) proceeded from his distillation
of an abundant language that he had previously completely mastered.

Rodin's drawings are relatively small in scale, usually within an area of ten by

Kneeling Girl. Pencil and watercolor,
12⅞″ × 9⅞″. The Art Institute of Chicago
(The Alfred Stieglitz Collection)

Reclining Nude. Pencil and watercolor,
10¼″ × 10⅜″. Collection
Mrs. Anne-Marie de Leur, New York

twelve inches—another fact often overlooked by present-day forgers. This may be explained by his practice of drawing without looking at the paper, which required him to keep his arm relatively stable but permitted free action to the wrist. The stability of the arm may have helped him to fix the proportion, scale and limits of the figure, for the position of his wrist and extension of his pencil would have kept him aware of its dimensions; at the same time, the freedom of the wrist would have allowed him to pursue his search for the great line with which to circumscribe the entire body without a break.

Absence of stylization helps to give Rodin's drawings an undated appearance, and their appeal to present-day eyes may also be due to certain contrasts with his least successful sculpture. The drawings never show any lapse of taste, any pretension, any synthesizing of figures or parts. In these private works he always sought the natural, but not the usual. Like the great corpus of his sculpture, Rodin's drawings present a bewildering richness; when they have all been made public, it will take years and generations of artists and historians to assimilate and recognize his range of ideas and esthetic, and assess their influence on such artists as Munch and Matisse. The danger that Rodin foresaw when his drawings were looked at in the future was that they would be appreciated solely in esthetic terms. "It is a false idea that drawing itself can be beautiful. It is only beautiful through the truths and the feelings that it translates." [13]

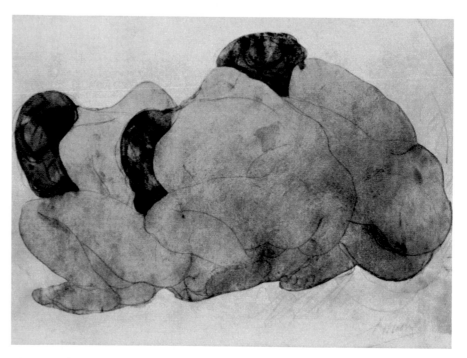

Three Crouching Women. Pencil and watercolor, 11⅛″ × 14⅞″. The Rodin Museum, Philadelphia

1. In her recent catalogue of the exhibition, "Rodin Inconnu," at the Louvre, Mme Gold-scheider dates the drawings inspired by Dante between 1880 and 1890. Since it is known that Rodin was deeply interested in Dante in 1875, it is highly probable that he made sketches from the *Inferno* before receiving the commission for *The Gates of Hell*. The various modes of drawings in this series suggest that their date should be extended back into the '70s rather than beginning with 1880.

2. In a future article, I propose to reproduce and comment on these drawings and deal at greater length with the origin and meaning of the series of *La Ronde*.

3. I owe thanks to my colleague Mark Musa, a Dante scholar, for the interpretation of this Canto.

4. The date of the group of drawings after Michelangelo in the Musée Rodin is unknown. They will be discussed by Albert Alhadeff in a forthcoming article on Rodin's early sculptures in the *Art Bulletin*. He argues against Grappe's dating of 1875, on the basis of Rodin's letter to his wife from Florence and a statement to Bartlett (*op. cit.*, p. 65); these indicate that the drawings related to the Medici Tombs which he made at that time were not sketched directly from them but were, rather, inspired by the impression that they made upon him. Rodin already knew these works from photographs, before his trip to Italy; evidence to support the argument that the surviving drawings represent student work will undoubtedly be supplied by Mr. Alhadeff (to whom I am also indebted for the photograph of the Loos Monument, p. 207).

5. They are reproduced in an article by P. Gsell, "Chez Rodin," *L'Art et les Artistes*, February, 1907, p. 49 and p. 51.

6. *On Art and Artists*, p. 114.

7. H. Lecoq de Boisbaudran, *Education de la mémoire pittoresque et la formation de l'artiste (Précédé d'une notice sur la vie de l'auteur, et d'une lettre d'Auguste Rodin)*, Paris, Laurens (n.d.), Preface.

8. *Ibid.*, p. 31.

9. Bartlett, *op. cit.*, p. 27.

10. Ludovici, *op. cit.*, pp. 138-39.

11. There are roughly seven thousand drawings in this archive, of which only about two hundred are exhibited in the museum and therefore available to the public. Among those to which access is not available are sketchbooks. Many of the unexhibited drawings are extremely fragile; however, there is not even a photographic record of these works to which scholars and artists can refer.

As this book goes to press, an important new study has appeared: Elisabeth Chase Geissbuhler, *Rodin; Later Drawings*, with interpretations by Antoine Bourdelle, Boston, Beacon Press, 1963. Besides including a number of hitherto unpublished drawings, the author, a student of Bourdelle's, has had access to much new material, including correspondence between Rodin and Bourdelle and the latter's "Private Notes on Rodin's Drawings," made in preparation for his article in *La Grande Revue* (January 10, 1908), reprinted in *La Sculpture et Rodin* (see bibl.).

12. *On Art and Artists*, p. 110.

13. *Ibid.*, p. 109.

Torso of a Young Woman. 1909. Bronze, 33¼″ high

THE PARTIAL FIGURE AND
THE FRAGMENT

THE ASPECT of Rodin's art that, after 1900, exerted the strongest influence on younger advanced sculptors such as Maillol, Matisse, Lehmbruck, Brancusi, Boccioni, Duchamp-Villon, Lipchitz and Archipenko was the partial figure—a torso or bodily extremities taken from an intact figure, so that the part substituted for the whole. Rodin's audacity in *exhibiting* these segments, beginning in 1898 with the headless *Study of a Seated Woman* (later given the title *Cybele*), dismayed the public, although it seems to have impressed some of the young sculptors.[1] The European museums of course were filled with fragments of ancient sculpture, and even the Paris Salons had accepted a partially finished figure, for example Bartholdi's large bust for the *Statue of Liberty* in 1878, though with the tacit understanding that the artist intended to bring the work to completion. Much of the public's indignation with Rodin after 1900 was because it felt that it was being denied the chance of seeing the artist's best work, which presupposed the total figure. To reduce adverse criticism, some of Rodin's friends explained in their writings that the master did indeed intend to complete some of his limbless torsos, such as the armless and headless *Walking Man*, but that he was concerned with not spoiling the ensemble. Contemporary newspaper reviews of these years, however, indicate that the fragments only confirmed the widespread suspicions aroused by the long delays of the projects for the *Balzac* and *Victor Hugo* monuments—namely, that Rodin was incapable of bringing his work to completion. Roger Fry commented in 1910 that for Rodin it was the unit that counted, not the unity: "Every part of the figure is instinct with the central idea, every detail of hand and foot is an epitome of the whole and the final composition of these parts is often a matter of doubt."[2] Degas reportedly asked Rodin: "Why did you make your *Walking Man* without head or arms?"; to which Rodin replied in a manner that explains their friendship: "Have you ever seen a man walk on his head? As for the arms, I preferred to have him walk on his legs like ordinary mortals—like you and me."[3]

p. 175

p. 30

This sculpture was given to the French Embassy in Rome in 1912 by a private committee that included Rodin's friends. It was set up in the courtyard of the Farnese Palace, but later rejected by the unhappy ambassador on the dubious grounds that it blocked traffic. The press was filled with quips from all sides, including the sculptor, concerning the appropriateness of a headless figure to symbolize the French Government's policy and the direction of its Embassy in Rome. *Charivari* wanted the sculpture to go to the Ministry of Foreign Affairs. In a sarcastic vein, Rodin was quoted: "My statue has no head. It is above all for this reason that the ambassador does not like it: a man without a head is a perfect symbol of our diplomacy."[4] Nevertheless Rodin was deeply wounded by the insult, and commented: "The head and arms are lacking. But that is of little importance to artists. It is in the business of making statues for five, two hundred or two thousand francs that one never forgets to put on the head and arms, and sometimes the hairs, one by one."[5] Even more than to the honor of having his sculpture in the Embassy at Rome, Rodin had initially responded with excitement to having *The Walking Man* in the courtyard of a palace designed in part by Michelangelo, and only after long meditation upon the sculpture and the architecture had he convinced himself that his work was worthy of its site. "My modeling belongs to those great architectural epochs that were antiquity and the Renaissance."[6]

Rodin often defended his partial figures by pointing out that neither the public nor the critics took offense at the sculptured bust, which was in truth a fragment. That antique torsos were publicly exhibited and used in art schools was also a precedent which undoubtedly gave the sculptor a strong incentive for exhibiting their equivalents. A statement he made in 1915 while in Rome, where he restudied ancient sculptural ruins, makes it evident that he saw his parts and fragments as finished works: "Beauty is like God; a fragment of beauty is complete."[7]

Although for many years Rodin had known the paintings and pastels of Degas, in which figures are intersected by the edges as in Japanese prints, it is hardly possible that these could have influenced him. Degas' segmentation of the figure results from the artist's fidelity to the way in which people and objects are seen in natural conjunction and close proximity. The cutting of Degas' figures is occasioned by their context in the world of objects and the limits of the field of perception. No such optical experience or principle determined Rodin's decision to divest his figures of certain parts.

The artist's habit of modeling parts of the body as separate and complete works dates back to his first attempts at sculpture while he was a student at the Petite Ecole. There, either upon the advice of an instructor or of his own accord, he set himself the task of mastering the parts of the human form before attempting the whole. Later, during the 1880s and '90s, when he could afford assistants such as Jules Desbois and Camille Claudel, he would instruct each of them to make, according to his particular talent, arms, hands, legs or feet in great supply, both for their own training and for his purposes. A description of Rodin's studio by one of his assistants is revealing:

> In the studio, for *The Gates of Hell* and other projected works, on tables, benches, chairs, on window sills, on the floor, were scattered or heaped designs and drawings, stood or lay fragments of sculptures in work, casts of all sorts, heads, torsos, arms and legs, detached dismemberings ready to be used or kept around because they might at some time prove suggestive.[8]

174

Today in the basement studio at Meudon are numerous vitrines filled with the sculptor's arsenal of *membra disjecta*. There are also many drawers carefully com- p. 176 posed with small or tiny hands, arms, legs and feet, that at first glance look like the present-day "accumulations" of Fernández Arman. It was above all his work on *The Gates* (in itself a gigantic fragment) that seems to have developed in Rodin the habit of treating the body like an assemblage of infinite variations. When figures were removed from the plaster frame of the door, they were cut off and stored on shelves. The artist early formed an acuity of judgment that enabled him to discern and separate the most expressive portions of his sculpture. His work was thus additive and subtractive. Some of the figures that were later enlarged and isolated from *The Gates*, for example certain versions

Study of a Seated Woman (Cybele). c. 1889. Bronze, 19¾" high

175

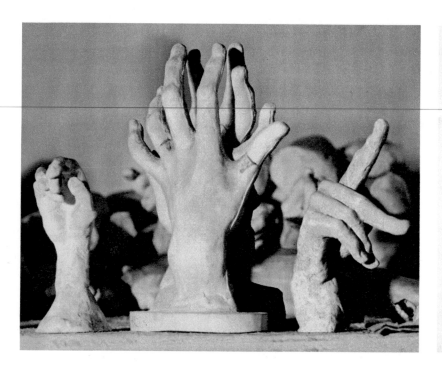

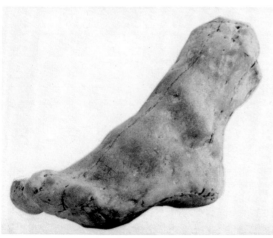

Above: Henri Matisse. *Study of a Foot.*
1900. Bronze, 12″ high

Below: Auguste Rodin. *Study of a Foot.*
Plaster, 3⅛″ high

Opposite page:

Above, left: *Studies of Hands.* Plaster

Above, right: *Hand.* c. 1885? Bronze,
3⅞″ high

Below: Drawer from Basement Studio
Meudon

p. 58, 59 and fragments of *The Crouching Woman*, still bear on their backs and heads the rough scars of this cutting away.

The detached head of *The Crouching Woman* has an intriguing double character. The left profile is generally smooth and firm in modeling, with the lowered eyelid, mouth and inclination of the head suggesting pathos. The opposite side still bears the cavities caused by the former pressure of the woman's knee. (When the head was joined to a new upright body and called *The Triton*, these marks for some unexplained reason still remained.)⁹ The upper part of the head displays a rugged inflection of masses and hollows in a location and sequence not clearly dictated by the woman's anatomy or coiffure. The expressiveness of the right profile does not rest upon a reading of the features but on the sculptor's arbitrary reworking of the head in a way that uncannily predicts the appearance, though not the principles, of the later cubist *Woman's Head* by Picasso and the busts by Matisse.

Head of "The Crouching Woman" ("La Luxure"). 1882. Bronze, 14¼" high

178

It is not known if these younger artists saw this work of Rodin's; but there is a comparison which shows both the influence of Rodin on Matisse, and the differences between the two. Matisse's making of a disembodied foot resulted *p. 177* from his exposure to the art of the older man. For Rodin, the appearance of the foot presented the challenge of an unexplored topography whose careful mapping could provide an object of wonder. Matisse, not content with objective imitation, was compelled to stress the design possibilities of the foot, de-emphasizing the flesh by altering its surface inflections through hard faceting and scraping with a knife and thus forcibly injecting his own personality and style into our consciousness of the object. Within the compact silhouette, he augmented the esthetic complexity by increasing the density of his modeling. In the final analysis, Matisse's handling appears subtractive compared with Rodin's building up of the form.

Even before he became Rodin's secretary in 1905 and 1906, Rainer Maria

Rilke had the opportunity of intimate access to the artist's thought and sculpture. In his first study on Rodin, written in 1903, the poet wrote:

> Completeness is conveyed in all the armless statues of Rodin: nothing necessary is lacking. One stands before them as before something whole. The feeling of incompleteness does not rise from the mere aspect of a thing, but from the assumption of a narrow-minded pedantry, which says that arms are a necessary part of the body and that a body without arms cannot be perfect.... Rodin, knowing through the education which he has given himself that the entire body consists of scenes of life, of a life that may become in every detail individual and great, has the power to give to any part of this vibrating surface the independence of a whole.[10]

His understanding of Rodin's isolation of hands was perfectly expressed:

> There are among the works of Rodin hands, single, small hands which, without belonging to a body, are alive. Hands that rise, irritated and in wrath; hands whose five bristling fingers seem to bark like the five jaws of a dog of Hell. Hands that walk, sleeping hands, and hands that are awakening; criminal hands, tainted with hereditary disease; and hands that are tired and will do no more, and have lain down in some corner like sick animals that know no one can help them....
> There is a history of hands; they have their own culture, their particular beauty; one concedes to them the right of their own development, their own needs, feelings, caprices and tendernesses.[11]

Such enlightened and sympathetic reading as Rilke's was, however, exceptional. During and after Rodin's lifetime, the view that he was perverted morally with respect to the body and to the public norms for sculpture had wide and lasting currency internationally. In a book written in 1925, Fred Wellington Ruckstull, an organizer of the National Sculpture Society in the United States, expressed this view:

> But why any man should, today, *deliberately model* a human body and then *mutilate it* and then *hack it*, and exhibit it, except as a revelation of his sadistic soul, passes our comprehension. The first man... to do this was Rodin – who was regarded in Paris as a moral sot. In his "Walking Man"... we have a glaring example. Here is the body of a man so skillfully modeled that he seems to live and walk, and the head and arms are *hacked off,* and the body otherwise mutilated.... To deliberately produce such a cadaver... and sell it, perhaps is proof of the working of a mind tainted with sadism.[12]

Such bitter denunciations gained support from a story that circulated widely in print after 1910 concerning an American woman who visited Rodin's studio to purchase a sculpture. The dialogue was reportedly as follows: "How much?" "Forty thousand francs." "All right, I'll buy it." "Wait!" Rodin, armed with a hammer, broke the legs, crushed the arms, smashed the nose and knocked off the ears. "Voilà!" "Never have I seen such a quick worker!"

Ironically, in commenting on Michelangelo's figures, including his broken sculptures, Rodin may have been revealing his own motivation: "All his statues are so constrained by agony that they seem to wish to break themselves. They all seem ready to succumb to the pressure of despair which fills them. When

Michelangelo was old, he actually broke them. Art did not content him. He wanted infinity."[13] Michelangelo and Rodin, like Brancusi and Giacometti, seem linked in that they established for their art standards of perfection so unattainable as to result in their reducing it by fragmentation or attrition.

GENERAL CHARACTERISTICS

If *The Walking Man* is correctly dated 1877–78, it would mark the beginning of Rodin's *pars pro toto* mode. Judging from the catalogue dates of his sculpture, the 1880s and early '90s (coinciding with his work on *The Gates*) would be the period when most of his figures were created through the process of amputation and reworking. Two major torsos date from after 1900. The following list gives the names and suggested dates for some of his partial figures and the complete figures to which they are related.[14] Only the headless *Seated Woman* and *The Earth* seem not to have been derived from some previous figure, while *The Walking Man* preceded a complete one:

p. 28

p. 38

> *The Walking Man*, 1877–78, ill. p. 28 (*St. John the Baptist Preaching*, 1878–80, ill. p. 29)
> *Torso of Adèle*, c. 1882, ill. p. 183 (Figure in *The Gates of Hell*, ill. p. 44)
> *Torso of a Man*, c. 1882, Grappe 82 (Falling Man in *The Gates*, c. 1882)
> *The Earth*, 1884, ill. p. 187
> *Meditation (The Inner Voice)*, c. 1885, Grappe 127 (Figure in *The Gates*)
> *Torso*, 1885–86?, ill. p. 79 (study for Pierre de Wiessant in *The Burghers of Calais*, c. 1886, ill. p. 71)
> *Seated Woman (Cybele)*, c. 1889, ill. p. 175
> *Flying Figure*, 1890–91, ill. p. 184 (*Avarice and Lust* in *The Gates*, c. 1887)
> *Iris, Messenger of the Gods*, c. 1890–91, ill. p. 185 (Muse for the *Monument to Victor Hugo*, 1890–91, Grappe 268)
> *Torso of a Young Woman*, 1909, ill. p. 172 (Figures in *The Gates*, 1880s)
> *Half-Length Figure of a Woman (Meditation)*, 1910, ill. p. 182 (*The Martyr*, 1884, ill. p. 153)

The truncation of parts was not due simply to the sculptor's whim, nor was it as indiscriminate as a first glance might suggest. He never cut a torso, head or extremity in half nor performed surgery at the joints. His knife was used at right angles to the long axis of the limb and often, as in the *Flying Figure*, at a point that permitted the stump to fuse with the body's silhouette. By reducing the body in this way, Rodin established a new authority of the artist over what had heretofore been considered the sanctity of the human form and the completeness of its external appearance, and gave sculpture a new integrity which (as Lipchitz has pointed out) was to influence cubist sculpture. He may have intended to show the body as marvelous and mysterious in every part and at the same time force the viewer's attention to the sculpture's execution. With *Iris, Messenger of the Gods* and the *Flying Figure*, the disposition of the limbs no longer gives the figure complete balance; the former requires an artificial vertical support to be seen upright, although in its original form (sometimes titled *Woman*

p. 176, 177

p. 184

p. 185

Half-Length Figure of a Woman (Meditation). 1910. Bronze, 27⅛" high

Doing the Split) the figure was self-supporting. In still another way, therefore, Rodin liberated the figure from the pedestal, by suspending it as if in a gravity-defying moment.

Whether Rodin consciously thought in these terms, the equilibrium of his pieces was more sculptural (as we use the word today) than anatomical or physiological, for he relied upon a balance based upon visual proportion and the interaction of shapes and masses of given weight and volume. Although Rodin seems never to have thought in completely abstract terms, what he was doing here with the figure was a precedent for the arbitrary proportioning of parts of the body for esthetic and expressive reasons, as it occurs after 1900 in the early art of Brancusi, Lehmbruck, Duchamp-Villon and others. Rodin gave these younger artists a precedent for establishing criteria and completeness that were

Torso of Adèle. 1882. Plaster, 17¾″ high × 6″ wide × 9¼″ deep

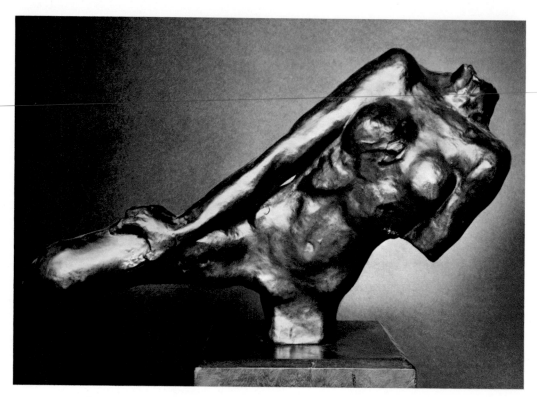

Flying Figure. c. 1890–91. Bronze, 20¾″ high × 30″ wide × 11¾″ deep

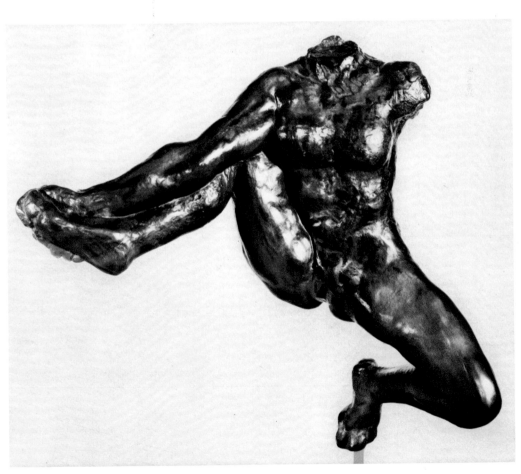

Iris, Messenger of the Gods. 1890–91. Bronze, 32⅛″ high × 33¼″ wide × 15¾″ deep

based upon the fragment's self-sufficient expressiveness and the sculpture's ability to be further curtailed without loss of its potency. His partial figures seemed to young artists a means of freeing sculpture from its literary ties (which ironically he had drawn heavily upon) and from the old rhetorical gestures and facial expressions. The fragments, however, often continued to suggest literary titles to Rodin, who once commented that literature, unlike sculpture, could convey such abstract ideas as *"Profound reflection often ends in inaction,* without the necessity of figuring a thoughtful woman held in a block of stone."[15] Yet there is a contradictory reference, shortly before, to the *Half-Length Figure of*

p. 182 *a Woman:* "Don't you see that I left it in that state intentionally? My figure represents *Meditation.* That's why it has neither arms to act nor legs to walk. Haven't you noticed that reflection, when persisted in, suggests so many plausible arguments for opposite decisions that it ends in inertia?"[16]

"THE EARTH"

In November, 1913, several Paris newspapers carried reports that Rodin had demanded confiscation of a work entitled *The Earth,* which a dealer named Moline claimed was by the sculptor. Some versions of the story related that Rodin had passed the gallery's window, stopped stupefied by the sight of his name attached to this sculpture, and thereupon summoned a bailiff to have the work and the dealer hauled into court. (The artist harbored a notorious dislike for dealers, choosing to sell all his work directly.) For many years before this incident he had been plagued by forgeries, some by the men to whom he had entrusted the making of his plaster casts. After 1900, many unscrupulous women who came into contact with Rodin used his fame and art for their own ends; one in particular, an American-born duchess, irresponsibly denounced works owned by dealers or private collectors as frauds, forcing the sculptor into embarrassing situations.

What seems to be the most reliable account of the affair of *The Earth* was that written by Claude Franceuil in *Gil Blas* (November 27, 1913). In this, it was stated that Rodin had not actually seen the bronze. The dealer traced the history of the piece back through six previous owners, the earliest being a German professor named Heilbuth who certified that he had bought *The Earth* from Rodin in 1898, and that the artist himself had inscribed on it *"premier épreuve."* Confronted with this evidence, and in all probability with the bronze itself (another cast of which had been in his exhibition in 1900), Rodin confessed: "The work is entirely mine... I freely confess my error." He would not be interviewed on the subject, and one of his entourage said that he could not understand why so unimportant a subject was being pursued. The press reveled in jokes about absent-mindedness and insincerity, and in parodies of the affair that included a skit in which *The Earth* played the son to Rodin's prodigal paternity.

The Earth. 1884. Bronze, 18¼″ high × 44½″ long × 15″ deep

Georges Grappe, the late curator of the Musée Rodin, cited evidence left by one of the sculptor's assistants that *The Earth* dated from about 1884, and that the artist had always been uneasy about it.[17] No specific reasons were given, but the fact that the work was exhibited only once, in 1900, seems to provide corroboration. Yet *The Earth* must rank with *The Walking Man* as among Rodin's most daring and moving sculptures. Seen for the first time, it may suggest a gigantic slug, a subhuman species still attached to primordial mud. It is an approximately recumbent human figure lacking feet and arms; what is unusual in Rodin's art is the undefined mass of the head. (In a smaller terra-cotta version at Meudon, Rodin attached to the body the head of *The Man with the Broken Nose*.) The sculpture is an inspired evocation of the earth as the source

p. 51 and ultimate destination of all life. By contrast with his Michelangelesque *Adam* a few years before, a man fully formed in God's image, this new Adam is a more personal conception of Rodin's. The emergence of life is now the outcome of a process that involves an irresistible power, not dependent on muscular energy, that separates, shapes and uplifts the body from the inchoate. During this raw genesis, the body is moved by blind instinct. No arms or feet offer visible leverage, no developed cranium directs the ascent. Seen from the side, the act of levitation appears to take place in sections, with the area of the shoulder and head the most elevated. Viewed from above, the body performs a serpentine movement, faintly echoing the back of the famous jaguar modeled by Rodin's teacher, Barye; it evokes the pitch and roll, twists and involuntary pulls that the new life requires to overcome the inertia of dead weight. Like an emerging massif or wave, the body projects rugged ridges, clefts and slides as unformed, extraneous matter slips from the nascent torso. (The lower part of the legs is not properly united with the upper section, seeming either too small or to have slipped out of joint. If this was a technical fault in the original clay or plaster, the artist made no attempt to conceal it in the bronze cast.)

More tellingly than any of Rodin's writings on comparative anatomy in nature, *The Earth* expresses his ideas about the mystical correspondences of growth that link all living matter. By its embodiment of the life urge, it complements the

p. 71 confrontation of a final return to the earth in *The Burghers of Calais* of the same period. The enactment of generation with its attendant convulsions and flux imparts poetic mystery to this most modern of Rodin's sculptures.

By substituting the test of esthetic and expressive validity for the conventional ideal of completeness, Rodin opened important avenues for the equivalence of form and meaning, through which the modern sculptor could make the human body correspond more completely to his own thought and feeling. The human body, which in violation of its traditional completeness and individuality Rodin often reduced to a fragment, nevertheless remained the object of his greatest wonder and respect, the means by which he could fulfil his life as

188

an artist. Through the body, he believed he could express all that was important in nature and the universe. This is the background for his statement on the artist's function:

> The artist, in representing the universe as he imagines it, formulates his own dreams. In nature, he celebrates his own soul. And so he enriches the soul of humanity. For in coloring the material world with his spirit he reveals to his delighted fellow beings a thousand unsuspected shades of feeling.... He gives them new reason for loving life, new inner lights to guide them.[18]

1. This is the earliest date given by Grappe for exhibition of any of the partial figures; they had been seen for many years earlier by countless visitors to Rodin's studio. The catalogue of the Rodin exhibition at the Galeries Georges Petit in 1889 lists several works as "*études*" or "*torses*," but since this catalogue is not illustrated it is difficult to say whether partial figures were included in this show. As this book goes to press, Leo Steinberg has called my attention to an interesting article on the origin and significance of Rodin's torsos and partial figures, which I have not yet had a chance to read: "Zur Genesis des Torso-Motivs und zur Deutung des fragmentarischen Stils bei Rodin," in *Das Unvollendete als künstlerische Form,* Ein Symposion, herausgegeben von J. A. Schmoll gen. Eisenwerth (Berne & Munich, Francke, 1959).

2. R. Fry, "The Sculptures of Maillol," *Burlington Magazine*, vol. XVII, April 1910, pp. 26 ff.

3. Frisch and Shipley, *op. cit.*, p. 311.

4. Article in *Cri de Paris*, January 8, 1937.

5. Article in *Intransigeant* (Paris), February 18, 1912.

6. Article in *Liberté* (Paris), February 19, 1912 (unsigned).

7. Cladel, *Rodin*, pp. 249-50.

8. Frisch and Shipley, *op. cit.*, p. 186.

9. A photograph of *The Triton* is reproduced on p.106 of the special issue of *L'Art et les Artistes,* 1914 (see bibl.).

10. R. M. Rilke, *Auguste Rodin,* English translation by Jessie Lemont and Hans Trausil, New York, 1948, pp. 24-25. Rilke was writing in part to counter charges against Rodin's "decadence," "pessimism," and especially his "incomplete execution" (with reference both to works such as the *Balzac,* and to the torsos) that were particularly current in Germany at the time; see U. Emde, *Rilke und Rodin,* Marburg/Lahn, 1949, pp. 96 ff.

11. *Loc. cit.* It is possible that Rilke may not have been discriminating between hands made by Rodin and those by his assistants, such as line the shelves in the basement of the museum at Meudon.

12. F. W. Ruckstull, *Great Works of Art,* New York, Putnam, 1925, p. 23.

13. *On Art and Artists,* pp. 228-29.

14. All dates are from Grappe, *op. cit.*

15. *On Art and Artists,* p. 168.

16. *Ibid.,* p. 164.

17. Grappe, *op. cit.,* p. 40.

18. *On Art and Artists,* pp. 181-82.

Edward Steichen. *Rodin – Le Penseur*. 1902. Pigment print

POSTSCRIPT:
RODIN AND AMERICA

VISITORS to the United States Centennial Exhibition in Philadelphia's Fairmount Park in 1876 could hardly have been impressed with the sculptures by Auguste Rodin.[1] The young artist, who had been working on decorative architectural commissions for the new Stock Exchange in Brussels, was represented by eight works among the Belgian entries. Except for the bust of a child, *Alsatian Orphan,* these have long since vanished, but their names – *Loving Thoughts, The Rose, Field Flowers* – give enough indication of their academic style and saccharine content. Yet they were made by the great genius who was to renew sculpture; who, after sculpture's position of despair in the nineteenth century, "succeeded in transforming everything," as Brancusi said; thanks to whom "sculpture became human again, both in its dimensions and spiritual content"[2]; and who was to become the most celebrated artist since Bernini.

One year after this exhibition took place, Rodin's first great masterpiece, *The Age of Bronze,* was shown in Paris. It shocked academic sculptors by its naturalism much as his later work was to arouse their antagonism for its audacity of form. A few Americans, however, recognized rather early the presence of a truly great artist. The now-obscure Boston sculptor, Truman H. Bartlett, visited Rodin in the mid-'80s and in 1889 published a detailed interview with him in some ten installments in the influential *American Architect and Building News,*[3] which has remained a principal source of biographical material on the artist. Wealthy business men and their wives had their portraits done by Rodin, though much of his other work offended the "prurient prudery of our puritanism."[4]

p. 20

In fact, when the French Government sent a number of Rodin's sculptures to Chicago's World Columbian Exposition in 1893, *The Kiss* and *Paolo and Francesca* were considered too lewd for public view, and in order to protect American morality the Fair officials isolated them in a special room where they could be seen only on individual application. The Art Institute of Chicago, however, acquired an important work at that time: the plaster of the magnificent *Jean d'Aire* from *The Burghers of Calais.* It was also in 1893 that The Metropolitan Museum of Art in New York acquired Rodin's *Head of St. John the Baptist,* the first of its large and significant collection of works by the sculptor.

Rodin's world-wide fame gained recognition by his special pavilion at the Paris Exposition Universelle in 1900. Whereas an American lady correspondent for a San Francisco newspaper considered the work she saw there "*cochonnerie*" and "degraded examples of the decadence of French art," calling the *Balzac* a "monstrous thing, ogre, devil and deformity in one,"[5] most American critics were aware of the significance of Rodin's work. They saw in it a combination of Phidias' heroic chisel and Dante's dramatic fantasy in a new sculptural form that continued the Renaissance-baroque tradition and simultaneously showed the possibilities of new development in sculpture "at the dawn of a new century."

The celebrated American dancer Loïe Fuller, whom Rodin admired because she had "awakened the spirit of antiquity, showing the Tanagra figurines in action,"[6] visited him in his "Temple" at Meudon and bought so much of his work that in September, 1903 the National Arts Club in New York was able to hold the first sizable exhibition of Rodin's sculpture in the United States, relying entirely on Miss Fuller's collection. It included plasters of the large *Age of Bronze, Adam, Eve* and *The Thinker*, bronze heads of *Victor Hugo* and *Balzac*, as well as Edward Steichen's photograph of *Rodin – Le Penseur*. The *New York Times* in an unsigned review quite rightly pointed out that "Rodin's work has a great deal of the quality of Wagner's music: it seizes one and carries one along despite all protests, it excites and disquiets one."[7]

Two years later the Copley Society of Boston combined the sculpture of Rodin with the painting of his contemporary Claude Monet (both artists were born in 1840) in an exhibition, as had been done by the Galerie Georges Petit in Paris in 1889. Eleven of Rodin's important works from four private collections were shown with considerable critical acclaim.

When the young American photographer Edward Steichen went to Paris in 1900, he made straight for the Rodin pavilion at the Exposition Universelle: "Rodin was the focal point of my trip."[8] It made a profound impression on him, and he was happy when the following year Fritz Thaulow, "the Norwegian painter of waterfalls"[9] offered to take him to Meudon to meet the great artist. Steichen still remembers with pride Rodin's comments about his portfolio and the master's invitation for Steichen to come to his studio whenever he wanted. Every Saturday for a year Steichen then bicycled from Paris up to Meudon where he "came under the inspiration of his grand and independent mentality and his extraordinary subtle perception of beauty."[10] In 1902 he photographed *p. 190* Rodin confronting his *Thinker* against the central background of the great marble *Victor Hugo*. This photograph, this "masterpiece of portraiture, an allegory, a document, virile, tender, a marching song without words,"[11] was, upon Rodin's suggestion, submitted with several others to the Salon at the Champs de Mars and accepted by the jury. If it had not been rejected by the more conservative Hanging Committee it would have been the first photograph ever to be shown in a Paris Salon.[12] In any case, it was immediately and widely shown all over Europe and America.

In 1905 Alfred Stieglitz together with Steichen established the Photo-Secession Gallery in Steichen's old studio at 291 Fifth Avenue. In keeping with the principle of showing not only photographs but all the arts, Steichen with the master's co-operation selected fifty-eight of Rodin's wash drawings for exhibition in New York. When they were shown at "291" in January 1908, a new

Edward Steichen. "*Balzac – Towards the Light, Midnight.*" Meudon, 1908

aspect of Rodin's genius became apparent. Stieglitz' avant-garde journal *Camera Work* quotes from eight reviews in New York newspapers. J. N. Laurvik in the *Times*, who saw in the wash drawings a challenge to American prudery, also considers the show "a hopeful sign of the changing order of things, when work such as this can be shown here in New York."[13] If the order did indeed change, it was largely due to Stieglitz and Steichen. Within a few years the Photo-Secession Gallery at "291" followed the Rodin show with the first American exhibitions of Matisse, Henri Rousseau, Cézanne, Picasso and Brancusi.

Not all the critics responded favorably to the Rodin drawings. Most of them were impressed with their vitality and spontaneity; the influential critic of the *Tribune,* Royal Cortissoz, remained skeptical, and a W. B. McCormick in the *Press* was offended: "Stripped of all 'art atmosphere' they stand as drawings of nude women in attitudes that may interest the artist who drew them, but which are not for public exhibition... they are most decidedly not the sort of thing to offer to public view in a gallery devoted even to preciosity in artistic things."[14]

Steichen returned to Paris and Meudon, and in September, 1908 Rodin had his plaster cast of the *Monument to Balzac* moved into the field overlooking the valley of Meudon during the full moon so that Steichen could photograph it with the moon as the sole source of light. Until dawn he photographed the great sculpture from all positions. Rodin paid Steichen the unheard-of sum of *p. 28* 1,000 francs (then $400) for the photograph, began calling him "*mon fils*" and gave him a bronze cast of the original version of *The Walking Man*, as "an admonition to keep on marching."[15] In 1910 the Little Galleries at "291" mounted a second exhibition of Rodin drawings—this time including the more carefully composed early line drawings, and in the following year *Camera Work* published a special Rodin issue illustrated with Steichen's photographs and superb collotype reproductions of the drawings (see bibl.). When Rodin was buried in Meudon in 1917, General Pershing appointed Edward Steichen to represent him at the funeral.

In 1906 Mrs. John W. Simpson, a friend of Steichen's, gave a fine cast of *The Age of Bronze* to The Metropolitan Museum of Art through its curator of painting, Roger Fry, a gift which was acknowledged with pleasure by Daniel Chester French, chairman of the Museum's Committee on Sculpture. A plaster cast of *The Thinker* had been presented to the Museum by the French Government two years earlier, after its showing at the Louisiana Purchase Exposition in St. Louis, and eventually *The Thinker* became a sort of trade-mark for the American art museum from coast to coast. In 1908 the Metropolitan's European agent advised its director, Edward Robinson, to purchase important pieces – especially marbles – from the artist before his death. In the ensuing correspondence between Robinson and Rodin, many of the letters from Paris were written for Rodin by his intimate friend and "muse," the Duchesse de Choiseul – originally Miss Coudert of New York. When in 1909 the American millionaire,

Thomas Fortune Ryan. 1909. Bronze, 22⅝" high

France. 1904. Bronze, 19⅝" high

194

Thomas Fortune Ryan, had his portrait made by Rodin the Duchessse de Choiseul persuaded him "to do something really worth-while for his country" by donating funds to the Metropolitan Museum for the purchase of works by Rodin. "By bringing over such works as those of Rodin and other masters," the duchess suggested, "the young American artists could have the best examples of Europe's greatest works amidst their own surroundings, and this would tend to build up a great American art," [16] an opinion confirmed a few years later by the great collector John Quinn. [17]

Mr. Robinson and Daniel Chester French then set out to select the work, and "in the summer of 1910, with the assistance of the sculptor, a choice was made at Rodin's studios in Paris and Meudon." [18] In 1912 the collection of sculptures by Rodin was opened officially by the Museum; it totaled thirty-two pieces, including eighteen signed plaster casts, made especially for the Metropolitan Museum by the sculptor from various clay studies, and donated by him to the Museum. Rodin himself was made an honorary fellow for life by the Metropolitan Museum and from that time on he referred to America's "Rodin Museum" and "Rodin Gallery" [19] in New York. Charles Newton Smiley began his review of this Rodin collection in the scholarly *Art and Archaeology:* "Since 1900 the art world has been learning to say Phidias, Michelangelo, Rodin...." [20]

It was also in 1912 that the States of New York and Vermont, in celebration of the tercentenary of the discovery of Lake Champlain, unveiled a monument to the great French explorer whose name it bears. At the base of the monument, as a gift of a French committee to the people of America on this occasion, was placed a bronze cast of Rodin's *France,* originally modeled in plaster in 1904 after Camille Claudel (and which had sometimes borne the alternative titles of *Byzantine Empress* and *Empress of the Roman Empire*).

At the Armory Show in 1913 Rodin was represented by seven drawings, lent by Gertrude Käsebier, who had made some fine portrait photographs of him in 1906 and 1907. [21] These drawings caused the academic painter and pompous critic, Kenyon Cox, to lump him with Matisse, the Cubists and the Futurists as one of the men "making insanity pay." [22] A few years later another critic considered the *Balzac* a "grotesque with a ghoulish, animalistic head" and the "appearance of a lewd and cruel ghost," [23] which was, after all, the feeling of the Société des Gens de Lettres when it refused to accept the monument in 1898. An anonymous writer in 1917 seemed to anticipate Hitlerian criticism when he published a brief article entitled "A Degenerate Work of Art," in which he expressed a most vociferous hostility to Rodin and the "brutal excrescence of his followers, many of whom are insane." [24] And as late as 1925, as Albert E. Elsen has noted (page 180), one of the founders of the National Sculpture Society speaks of Rodin as a "moral sot" and cites the fact that the head and arms of *The Walking Man* were missing – or "hacked off" – as clear proof that the sculptor's

p. 212

mind was "tainted with sadism."[25] His view typifies that of this reactionary group of American sculptors.

A less belligerent attitude was expressed in an article in the *Metropolitan Museum of Art Bulletin* on the American sculpture of the day, which had nothing but praise for pieces by other artists, entitled *Duck-Baby, Happy Tiger, and End of the Trail*. The author's conclusions were probably quite typical of conservative American opinion: "However deeply our sculptors have felt Rodin's power, the fact remains that for the most part they have been touched by the characteristic beauties of his style rather than by his equally characteristic ugliness. These last were, of course, part and parcel of his living faith, but as articles of creed, they are not wholly convincing to our sculptors. Our art has no harvest of *Vieilles Heaulmières*, not because we deny Villon and Rodin, but because such a crop is foreign to the genius of our soil."[26] We may wonder today whether Theodore Dreiser and Thomas Eakins were also "foreign to our soil," but critics like Miss Adeline Adams preferred to concentrate on the positive side of life on the new continent. One of America's most noted sculptors of the day, Lorado Taft, reviewing Rodin's contributions in a lecture at the Art Institute of Chicago, spoke with great admiration for the sculptor, though he perceived "childish and senile fancies" in his more "extravagant work."[27] Actually, the conservative Taft utilized Rodin's formal innovations in his own works, but substituted flamboyant sentimentality for Rodin's genuine feeling.

It was shortly before the outbreak of the First World War that Mrs. Alma de Bretteville Spreckels of San Francisco met Loïe Fuller in New York, initiating a friendship which was to last until the latter's death in 1928. Later in the summer of 1914 the veil dancer took Mrs. Spreckels to meet Rodin in Meudon, where, according to his American student Malvina Hoffman, who was present at that meeting, the two ladies tried to persuade Rodin to come to America. While the seventy-four-year-old sculptor refused to make this long trip, he was happy to sell important pieces of sculpture to Mrs. Spreckels, including casts of *St. John the Baptist Preaching*, *The Prodigal Son*, *The Age of Bronze*, and the bust of Rochefort. At about this time Rodin also had his *Thinker* shown at the Panama-Pacific International Exposition of 1915 (it seems that no international fair was complete without this imposing sitter); the sculpture was promptly bought by Mrs. Spreckels and sent to Maybeck's romantic Palace of Fine Arts together with other large bronzes. By the time Rodin died in 1917, Mrs. Spreckels owned eighteen of his works, undoubtedly constituting the largest private collection of his sculpture on this side of the ocean. She and Loïe Fuller[28] then decided that an appropriate museum should be built, and during a ride through the magnificent Lincoln Park overlooking the Golden Gate, they selected a beautiful site in which a replica of the Paris building of the Legion of Honor was to be erected. *The Thinker* was placed as the centerpiece for the

The Three Shades. 1880. Bronze, 74$\frac{1}{4}$" high on base 71" long × 30" deep
Lincoln Park, San Francisco

Court of Honor, The California Palace of the Legion of Honor, San Francisco

The Rodin Museum, Philadelphia

Court of Honor of the new building. Between 1932 and 1950 Mr. and Mrs. Spreckels donated to the new California Palace of the Legion of Honor thirty-six bronzes, all cast before the master's death, as well as thirty-four plasters, five marbles, one terra cotta and nine drawings.

p. 197   In the early '20s Rodin's impressive *Three Shades* was placed across the road from The California Palace of the Legion of Honor as a memorial to Raphael Weill. Years later this monumental sculpture was selected by San Francisco Republican leaders to be reproduced on the cover of the program for their 1956 Presidential Convention, to illustrate Peace, Progress and Prosperity. The program cover was abandoned very quickly when it was discovered that the figures were originally the guardians who stand over the lintel of *The Gates of Hell*.

Jules E. Mastbaum of Philadelphia had a small collection of bronzes, including some works by Rodin's teacher Barye, before he went to Paris in 1924. There the Michigan-born painter Gilbert White took him to the Musée Rodin at the Hôtel Biron. Mastbaum persuaded the curator to allow him to buy a small bronze bust which he took back to Philadelphia.

Mastbaum's enthusiasm for Rodin grew quickly and, being a highly civic-minded individual, he proposed to build a Rodin Museum for the City of Philadelphia. The French Art Commission allowed the most important pieces, representing every phase of Rodin's work, to be cast by the firm of Alexis Rudier, who had worked with Rodin during his lifetime. The architect Jacques Gréber of Paris, who had originally studied painting with Redon and

Emile Bernard, collaborated with Paul P. Cret of Philadelphia in designing a building inspired by the Château d'Issy, whose doorway Rodin had bought and removed to his studio at Meudon; the white limestone for the Rodin Museum in Philadelphia was shipped from the Ile de France.

His friend Gilbert White related that "Mr. Mastbaum made arrangements… for the rebuilding of Rodin's studio in Meudon, which is falling into ruin from neglect. He is also presenting a museum to be built there, which will contain the maquettes and sketches which at present are not on view."[29] As hundreds of original plasters and drawings had been inadequately protected, Mr. Mastbaum presented the Government of France with a securely restored building to house the treasures at Meudon; it is regrettable that his family has never received proper acknowledgment of his generosity from the French authorities. He also ordered the first two bronze casts to be made from the plaster *Gates of Hell*, one for the Musée Rodin in Paris and one to be installed in front of the Rodin Museum on the Parkway in Philadelphia. On November 29, 1929, three years after Mastbaum's death, the Rodin Museum of Philadelphia opened to the public. At the dedication New York's mayor, Jimmy Walker, shared the platform with Paul Claudel, the French Ambassador to the United States. The Museum houses a great collection of eighty-five bronzes, thirty-nine plasters, sixty-four drawings, and two paintings, as well as important letters and ephemera.

On the occasion of the opening of the Rodin Museum in Philadelphia, Francis Henry Taylor, then curator of medieval art at the Pennsylvania Museum,[30] felt that the *Gates of Hell* belonged in "the category of conscious classics of 1900."[31] Indeed Rodin was already considered *passé*. The Museum itself suffered a temporary decline in attendance: "now only a handful of persons, fewer than fifty a day, and only an occasional Philadelphian, visit the beautiful Rodin Museum,"[32] reads a newspaper report of 1936.

Artists and critics in the '20s, '30s and '40s no longer felt threatened by Rodin's violence and expressionist audacity, nor did they significantly respond to his work. Except for an occasional nod in the direction of "the originator of modern sculpture," he was ignored, although the general public continued to admire *The Thinker, The Hand of God* and especially *The Kiss*. From 1929 until 1942 the *Art Index* shows no critical article on Rodin in any American publication. The sculptor who had placed such great emphasis on the interaction of his hands and tools with the clay that they modeled gave rise to a generation of artists who made such a fetish of "truth to the material" that they expected the material "to speak for itself." They no longer had much use for Rodin's complex bronze casts, and even less for his marbles, many of which, to be sure, had been carved by assistants. The fact that thought and emotion–rather than the material itself–inspired his work caused the new generation to denigrate him as a "literary" artist. Joseph Hudnut, who was later to become Dean of Archi-

tecture at Harvard, typically misinterpreted *The Burghers of Calais* as "the supreme example of this literature-sculpture. To convey an intense emotional
feeling Rodin is literal in his description of the effects of emotion upon body and
face. But without the story the group is meaningless, is without power....
Thought and feeling... shatter in Rodin all formal beauty," Hudnut goes on to
observe, and "the extreme example of this destructive effect of thought and
feeling on form is in the *Balzac*," where "even the stone (*sic*) disappears in the
intense vibration of light".[33]

Clive Bell had taught that the essence of art lies in "significant form"; his
followers mistook this for "simple form" and looking at Rodin's sculpture,
where each inch of nervous surface has the life of a passionate gesture, these
purists were bewildered. They found neither stable structure nor structural
stability. Searching for new principles of plastic form, they found too much
individualism. Longing for the severity of archaic sculpture, they were ashamed
to be descendants of the baroque. And the purists agreed with an older generation of moralists in condemning Rodin's sensuous nudes: if they were danger-
ous morally for the older generation, they were too cluttered with irrelevant
associations for the younger one, who wanted their form "pure and simple."
But, while sculptural form is truly significant in Rodin, his sculptures are never
mere arrangements of formal elements.

In 1949, Albert E. Elsen began intensive historical research on Rodin under the
guidance of Professor Meyer Schapiro at Columbia University, resulting in a
preliminary article in *Magazine of Art* in 1952 and his probing and extensive
study of the sources and evolution of *The Gates of Hell*,[34] as well as in the present
monograph. Now new scholarly research is under way by American students of
Rodin's work. It is to be hoped that the essential archival material at the Hôtel
Biron and the actual sculptural studies at Meudon may soon become fully accessible to scholars throughout the world.

Surely the most important contribution to the new appreciation of Rodin in
America was made by Jacques Lipchitz and his friend Curt Valentin, the gallery director who introduced modern sculpture to a broad American public.
Not long after coming to the United States in 1937 as director of the New York
branch of Berlin's Buchholz Gallery, Curt Valentin at Lipchitz' suggestion
showed work by Rodin in his exhibitions entitled "From Rodin to Brancusi"
(1941) and "Homage to Rodin" (1942), as well as in shows of his drawings and
watercolors.[35] Now that sculpture was at last beginning to be widely recognized
as a major art form in this country, Valentin felt that it was time to introduce
the public to one of the major sources of modern sculpture itself. In May, 1954
the Curt Valentin Gallery opened a major Rodin exhibition of forty-four
sculptures and thirty-seven drawings, a show which had been in preparation for
many years. The gallery was crowded with visitors, many of whom experienced

Edward Steichen. *Rodin's "Monument to Balzac" in the Sculpture Garden of The Museum of Modern Art, New York.* 1955. Photograph

their first encounter with the work of the great master. Lipchitz, Jean Arp and André Masson wrote contributions for the catalog, which included excerpts from Rodin's own writings and from a perceptive letter by Rilke.

Howard Devree began his review of the exhibition in *The New York Times* by stating: "As time adds perspective to our view it may well be that those critics will be justified who have called Cézanne and Rodin the two giants of the nineteenth century."[36] A few years earlier, Andrew Carnduff Ritchie in his book, *Sculpture of the Twentieth Century*, written to accompany The Museum of Modern Art's exhibition which included five of the artist's sculptures, had asserted: "Rodin is the father of modern sculpture, and probably the greatest sculptor of our day. While his principal work was done in the last quarter of the nineteenth century his influence on modern sculpture has probably been more profound than any other."[37] Leo Steinberg, reviewing this book, reveals one important aspect of this influence: "Rodin does belong to us; not by virtue of his light-trap modelling, but because in him, for the first time, we see firm flesh resolve itself into a symbol of perpetual flux.... The sculptor studying not states of being, but forms of transition–this is the common factor that unites Rodin's *Defense*, Picasso's cubist *Head*, Gabo's *Spiral Theme*, and Roszak's *Spectre of Kitty Hawk*."[38] Although Rodin's work had been around for half a century, it began to be seen with fresh eyes in the '50s. There was now a general predisposition in the direction of his freedom of form, his exuberance of content, and even his "painterly" sculpture, so dependent upon effects of light. And new artists no longer considered thought and feeling destructive of form.[39]

p. 29   In January, 1955 the first sculpture by Rodin, his *St. John the Baptist Preaching*, entered the permanent collection of The Museum of Modern Art,[40] serving "both as a fundamental basis for comparison and point of departure"[41] for
p. 88   modern sculpture. A few months later the *Monument to Balzac* was formally presented to The Museum of Modern Art as a memorial to Curt Valentin, who had died the previous August. One hundred and thirty friends had raised the funds for this monumental nine-foot-high sculpture which was installed permanently in the Museum's Sculpture Garden. In accepting the *Monument to Balzac* for the Museum, Alfred H. Barr, Jr. called it "the unique climax of (Rodin's) mature style. With the bold modeling, dramatic pose and overwhelming power of the *Balzac,* Rodin may be said to have initiated expressionist tradition in modern sculpture. And quite aside from its importance as a pioneer work, the *Balzac* should take its rightful place as one of the very great sculptures in the entire history of Western art."[42]

p. 201   Edward Steichen, then Director of the Museum's Department of Photography, photographed the great bronze a second time. But unlike the famous pictures he had taken at Meudon forty-seven years earlier, this one was taken in the full light of day.

PETER SELZ

1. I wish to express my gratitude to those who have helped to unearth material on Rodin and America: Thomas C. Howe, Lucy Lippard, Henri Marceau, Grace M. Mayer, John Goldsmith Phillips, Gaillard F. Ravenal, Mrs. Charles J. Solomon, Capt. Edward Steichen, Mrs. Jane Wade Lombard, Mrs. Acey Wolgin.

2. Constantin Brancusi, "Hommage à Rodin," Quatrième Salon de la Jeune Sculpture, Paris, Gizard, 1952.

3. See bibl.

4. J. N. Laurvik in *New York Times*, quoted in *Camera Work*, no. 22, April, 1908, p. 36.

5. Quoted in Frederick Lawton, *The Life of Auguste Rodin*, New York, Scribner, 1907, p. 235.

6. Loïe Fuller, *Fifteen Years of a Dancer's Life*, Boston, Small Maynard & Co., 1913, p. 127.

7. *The New York Times*, September 5, 1903.

8. Edward Steichen, interview with the author, July 25, 1962.

9. *Ibid.*

10. Charles H. Caffin, *Camera Work*, no. 2, 1903, pp. 22-23.

11. Carl Sandburg in *Steichen the Photographer*, texts by Carl Sandburg, Alexander Liberman, Edward Steichen and René d'Harnoncourt, biographical outline by Grace M. Mayer, New York, The Museum of Modern Art, 1961, p. 25.

12. *Ibid.*, p. 70.

13. J. N. Laurvik, *loc. cit.*

14. Quoted in *Camera Work*, no. 22, April, 1908, p. 40.

15. Steichen, interview with the author, November 29, 1962.

16. Herman Bernstein, *Celebrities for Our Time*, New York, Lawren, 1924, pp. 122-23.

17. John Quinn, "Sculpture of the Exhibition," *Arts and Decoration*, Nov., 1913, p. 17.

18. Joseph Breck, *The Collection of Sculptures by Auguste Rodin*, New York, The Metropolitan Museum of Art, 1913, p. 3.

19. Bernstein, *loc. cit.*

20. "Rodin in The Metropolitan Museum," *Art and Archaeology*, vol. III, no. 2, February, 1916, p. 107.

21. The catalog of the Armory Show also lists a bronze "Figure of a Man," but Walt Kuhn wrote in a letter that no sculpture by Rodin was in the exhibition.

22. *The New York Times*, March 16, 1913.

23. Charles L. Borgmeyer, "Among Sculptures—Auguste Rodin," *Fine Art Journal*, vol. XXXII, 1915, p. 190.

24. "A Degenerate Work of Art—A Woman in Contortion by Rodin," *The Art World*, Nov., 1917, p. 130.

25. See pp. 180, 189 n. 12.

26. Adeline Adams, "Contemporary American Sculpture," *Metropolitan Museum of Art Bulletin*, vol. XIII, no. 4, April, 1918.

27. Lorado Taft, *The Scammon Lectures*, The Art Institute of Chicago, 1917, p. 21.

28. Loïe Fuller was also instrumental in introducing Samuel Hill to Auguste Rodin, and Mr. Hill was unquestionably encouraged further by Mrs. Spreckels in his enthusiasm for the sculptor's work. Between 1915 and 1922 Samuel Hill bought a great many plasters, some fine bronzes, terra cottas and drawings from Rodin, and after the artist's death from Loïe Fuller. This considerable collection was donated by Mr. Hill to the Maryhill Museum of Fine Arts in Maryhill, Washington, of which he was the founder and of which Mrs. Alma de Bretteville Spreckels is still Honorary Chairman.

29. "Musée Rodin de Philadelphie, Fondation Mastbaum," *Renaissance de l'Art Français*, vol. 9, no. 10, November, 1926, p. 600.

30. The Pennsylvania Museum of Art was until 1938 the name of the Philadelphia Museum of Art, which administers the Rodin Museum.

31. "Rodin," *Parnassus*, Feb., 1930, p. 10.

32. Robert Reiss in the *Philadelphia Record*, June 14, 1936.

33. Joseph Hudnut, *Modern Sculpture*, New York, Norton, 1929, pp. 24-25.

34. Albert E. Elsen, "Genesis of Rodin's Gates of Hell," *Magazine of Art*, vol. 45, March, 1952, pp. 110-19; *Rodin's Gates of Hell*, Minneapolis, University of Minnesota Press, 1960.

35. The name of the Buchholz Gallery was officially changed to Curt Valentin Gallery in 1951. Works by Rodin were included in the following exhibitions at this gallery: "From Rodin to Brancusi: European Sculpture of the Twentieth Century," February 11-March 8, 1941 (6 works by Rodin); "Homage to Rodin: European Sculpture of Our Time," Nov. 10-Dec. 5, 1942 (9 works by Rodin); "Auguste Rodin. Watercolors and Drawings," Oct. 2-26, 1946 (60 works); "The Heritage of Auguste Rodin. An Exhibition Assembled in Honor of the Diamond Jubilee of the Philadelphia Museum of Art," Dec. 6, 1950-Jan. 6, 1951 (6 works by Rodin); "Auguste Rodin," May 4-29, 1954.

36. "The Giant Rodin," *The New York Times*, May 9, 1954.

37. *Sculpture of the Twentieth Century*, New York, Museum of Modern Art, 1953, p. 14.

38. "Sculpture Since Rodin," *Art Digest*, August, 1953, p. 22.

39. Hudnut, *loc. cit.*

40. From 1941 to 1945 another cast of this sculpture from the collection of Dr. Michael Berolzheimer had been on loan to The Museum of Modern Art. This cast was acquired by the City Art Museum of St. Louis in 1945.

41. Alfred H. Barr, Jr., quoted in a Museum of Modern Art press release, January 18, 1955.

42. *Idem*, release dated March 4, 1955.

1840 November 12: François-Auguste-René Rodin born in the old twelfth district of Paris, to Jean-Baptiste Rodin, an employee of the Prefecture of Police, and his wife, the former Marie Cheffer; their daughter, Maria, had been born in 1838. He is given a religious upbringing, attending a Catholic school until 1849. At nine begins to draw, using scraps of paper discarded by his mother after they have been used as wrappings for groceries.

1851- Sent to his uncle's boarding school at Beauvais,
1854 but proves to be a poor student, which some biographers have attributed partly to myopia. Continues drawing; by the time of return to Paris in 1853, has decided to be an artisan.

1854- Enrolled at the "Petite Ecole" (the Ecole Im-
1857 périale Spéciale de Dessin et de Mathématiques, now the Ecole Supérieure des Arts Décoratifs), of which he is later to comment: "They had preserved a little of the eighteenth century... good antique models and excellent teachers. The three years at the Petite Ecole were the germinating of my life, where my own nature planted itself on firm ground without hindrance... where I received the only instruction of my life" (Bartlett, see bibl., p. 27). Fellow-students include the painters Legros and Cazin who become lifelong friends. His most important instructor is Horace Lecoq de Boisbaudran, originator of a highly effective system to train the artist to draw from memory and insure his individuality (pages 160-62); he also has his charges draw from Boucher, Bachelier, Bouchardon and Carel Van Loo, which conditions the young Rodin's taste and drawing style to that of the eighteenth century. Further studies at the Louvre and the Galerie des Estampes de la Bibliothèque Impériale, where he encounters engravings of the work of Raphael and Michelangelo, and studies L'Histoire du costume romain for drapery. At fifteen, receives a bronze medal for drawing from casts and is admitted to the class of a sculptor named Fort. His first efforts are clay figure studies. In the evenings, studies the nude model under a teacher named Lucas at the Gobelins factory. At seventeen, is awarded the school's first-class bronze medal for modeling and a second-class medal for drawing from casts. Attends courses in literature and history at the Collège de France, from which time date his first readings in Michelet, Hugo, Musset, Lamartine and Dante. In 1857, his drawings are seen and praised by the sculptor Hippolyte Maindron, who advises him to enter the Ecole des Beaux-Arts.

1857- Tries unsuccessfully three times at six-month
1858 intervals to be admitted as a sculpture student in the "Grande Ecole" (Ecole des Beaux-Arts); his drawings are accepted, but he fails to pass the sculpture examination, as his eighteenth-century manner does not accord with his examiners' classical tastes. This rejection is a serious blow, as graduation from the School is essential for obtaining acceptance at the Salons and important public commissions. Begins taking on odd jobs, including working in 1857 for a decorator who in turn is doing jobs under Viollet-le-Duc, at this time restoring Nôtre-Dame.

1858- Continues with a succession of odd jobs, in-
1862 cluding such menial tasks as mixing plaster, removing mould marks, and making papier-mâché casts for forty cents a day but meanwhile thoroughly learning his craft. Between 1858 and 1860, works with a plasterer named Constant Simon, who, he says later, teaches him "the science of modeling" by showing him how to model a subject in depth. In 1860 after three years of work finishes his earliest surviving sculpture, a portrait of his father (page 108). In 1861 and 1862, in the employ of decorators named Blais, Cruchet and Legrain, apparently learns to carve stone and also to work with precious stones.

1862- The death of his beloved sister Maria, who had
1863 taken vows to be a nun, induces a severe crisis. Christmas, 1862, enters the Order of the Fathers of the Holy Sacrament as Brother Augustin. His abilities are recognized by the founder of this Order, Père Pierre-Julien Eymard, who encourages him to continue in sculpture by having a bust of himself made and who, although objecting to the "hornlike" treatment of the hair and refusing to reimburse the artist for his work, orders copies made (pages 108, 131 n. 7). Leaves the Order; rents a stable in the rue de la Reine Blanche where he begins eighteen months of work on The Man with the Broken Nose (page 106). Follows Barye's courses in animal anatomy at the Museum of Natural History. Enjoys brief membership in a club where he meets Théophile Gautier and Dumas père and encounters Carpeaux, whom he later recalls as having been cold toward him and his work. To support himself, works during the daytime for an ornament-maker named Bies and a jeweler, Fanières; obtains brief employment involving some stone-cutting from a friend in Marseilles and goes to Strasbourg to work in the Gothic style for a marchand de bons dieux.

1864- Makes his first attempt to exhibit by submitting
1866 to the Salon of 1864 his plaster of The Man with the Broken Nose (entitled "Mask" because the back of the clay head has fallen off during a cold spell), but it is rejected (pages 109-10). Works on several decorative assignments, including cary-

atids for the Gobelins Theater, a chimney ornamentation for the Gaîté-Lyrique Theater, a pediment for the Panorama des Champs-Elysées and decorative reliefs for the Salle de Rubens in the Louvre. Works for a few months without pay for the sculptor Chapu. Through a photographer named Aubry, meets Ernest Carrier-Belleuse (1824-87), much admired by Tuileries society and called the *Petit Maître* of the Second Empire. Although still working for Fanières, also goes to work part-time under Carrier-Belleuse's direction at the Sèvres porcelain factory. While working for the Gobelins Theater in 1864 meets Rose Beuret, then employed as a seamstress; she becomes Rodin's mistress and remains with him faithfully until her death in 1917, posing frequently as his model and devotedly assisting him by keeping the clay moist to prevent its cracking in the unheated studios. She poses for a major work, *The Bacchante*, on which he works for three years but which is accidentally broken in the course of being moved to another studio about 1866; he once describes this lost work by saying: "In style and modeling it was like *The Broken Nose*, and better than *The Age of Brass* (*sic*). Very firmly modeled, possibly a little cold" (Bartlett, see bibl., p. 28). Constantly works from the model and attends the Salons to compare his progress with that of established sculptors of the time; also has in his studio plaster casts of ancient sculpture, including the *Venus de Milo* and the *Dying Gladiator*.

1866- In 1866, Rose bears a son, to whom the father
1870   gives only his first name. (Auguste-Eugène

Alsatian Woman (Rose Beuret). c. 1890.
Terra cotta, 20⅞" high

Beuret, died 1934, becomes a mediocre printmaker and never fulfils his father's hopes for his success in art, and no warm relationship between the two is ever established, though the son poses for such sculptures as *The Burghers of Calais*.) A number of works done before 1870, including a small statue of the Virgin, a gladiator, and an amor, are mentioned in letters to Rose; these and many others seemingly lost owing to lack of funds for adequate studios and the means to preserve them.

1870- During the Franco-Prussian War, is enrolled in
1871   the 158th Regiment of the National Guard, serving in Paris and attaining the rank of corporal; makes at least two portrait busts of officers in the battalion. Discharged for poor health in 1871. During the Commune, lack of employment for artists and craftsmen causes him to look elsewhere. Goes to Brussels—according to some accounts, en route to England for a planned trip; according to others, at the invitation of Carrier-Belleuse. Works only briefly for Carrier-Belleuse, who makes a considerable amount of money from his assistant's work but becomes jealous of his attempts to sell his works independently. Collaborates for a short period with little financial success with another artist, Julien Dillens. Rose and the young Auguste are meanwhile left behind in Paris, enduring severe privation; his mother also dies during his absence from Paris.

1872   By working alone at night and saving money, he is able to hire a stone carver to make a marble version of *The Man with the Broken Nose*, which he sends to the Brussels Salon (and which is later accepted under the title of *Portrait of M. B—* at the Paris Salon of 1875).

1873- In February, 1873, enters into partnership with
1874   a former Belgian employee of Carrier-Belleuse, Joseph van Rasbourgh, supposedly for twenty years but actually lasting only until August 31, 1877. In theory each sculptor is to sign the work destined for his respective country, but actually van Rasbourgh, although of little value to the partnership, signs all Rodin's work. Among the sculptures produced in Brussels by the "partnership" are groups of *Amors Presenting Trophies* and *Arts and Sciences*, for the Palais des Académies on the rue Ducale; about ten caryatids for buildings on the Boulevard Anspach, some of which are now in the Musée Rodin (page 16); and pediment groups for the exterior and caryatids for the interior of the Stock Exchange. Two miniature busts, *Suzon* and *Dosia*, are bought for a small sum by a Belgian firm, with rights for their infinite reproduction, and are sold by the hundreds in Belgium. A number of terra-cotta figures, sold at the Albert Hall in London by an English dealer, are seen and admired there by Dalou. In the Forest of Soignes

Sailor (detail of *Loos Monument*). 1874.
Stone. Antwerp

paints several small, Corotlike sketches (now in the Musée Rodin); reads and reflects on his art; makes portraits of several friends, including the sculptors Paul de Vigne, De Winne, Boure, Constantin Meunier and the engraver Gustave Biot. Rose, who has rejoined him, later recalls these years as the happiest period of their union. In 1874 is invited with his erstwhile partner to go to Antwerp to make a commemorative monument to a Burgomaster, J. F. Loos, for a wealthy patron, Jules Pecher, a ship-owner with aspirations to be a sculptor, who with the artist's permission signs his own name to the finished work. Despite the changes, conniving, and miserliness of this patron, he tries to make this work in the style of Rubens, "hardy and vigorous"; years later, he tells Bartlett: "I worked on those figures with the greatest ardor from a decorative point of view, and it was while I was making the figure of the sailor that I was struck with its resemblance to the statues of Michelangelo, though I had not had him in mind. The impression astonished me, and I wondered what should cause it.... My studies had been a blind search after the movement of figures, and in making this one, I was, for the first time, impressed with its resemblance to the compositions of the great Florentine.... To satisfy my mind of the reality of this resemblance and to confirm my hope of its depth and value, either as the result of long years of effort, or as the effect of my admiration for him, I made a lot of sketches to see if I could get the same character, but without success" (Bartlett, see bibl., p. 45).

1875–
1876
At the end of the winter 1874-75 sets out on a two-month trip for a first visit to Italy to study Michelangelo in the original, traveling through Reims, Turin, Genoa, Pisa, Florence and Rome. Excited by Donatello. Spends a week studying Michelangelo's Tombs in the Sacristy of San Lorenzo and making sketches in the evenings in his room "not of his works but of figures... imagined and elaborated in order to understand his technique" (letter to Rose, quoted in Cladel, *Rodin*, p. 45). On his return to Brussels, the immediate consequences of this trip are possibly the "Ugolino group" referred to in biographies, and the beginning of work on *Adam*—which, however, is interrupted for several years. Begins work on what in 1877 is to become known as *The Age of Bronze*, choosing as his model a soldier telegrapher from a nearby barracks; works first on about one-third life-size scale, then half life-size, completing the sculpture in December 1876 (pages 20–26). According to Charbonneau, also begins *The Walking Man* in this year, perhaps indirectly inspired by casts from fragments of antique sculptures in the Museum of Comparative Sculpture in Brussels.

1877
Exhibits *The Age of Bronze* under its original title, *The Vanquished*, at the January Exposition du Cercle Artistique in Brussels. The work is admired but also draws the insinuation from some critics that it has been made at least in part from life casts, a charge that persists when it is shown in the May Salon at the Palais des Champs-Elysées in Paris, where he lists himself in the catalogue for the only time as a student of Barye and Carrier-Belleuse. On the advice of the sculptor E. Guillaume, he writes Rose to have a cast and photographs made of the model in Brussels in order to refute the charge, but this evidence is ignored by the Salon jury (page 21). Although poorly situated in the Salon, the sculpture attracts considerable attention and creates a sensation among students of the Ecole des Beaux-Arts. By Autumn, he has returned permanently to Paris with Rose, presumably to develop further his ideas for *The Walking Man* and begin *St. John the Baptist Preaching*. Before leaving Brussels, sends to London a sketch for a monument to Lord Byron, of which no trace remains.

1878–
1880
Is obliged to continue devoting most of his time to earning his livelihood by commercial art, doing decoration for furniture and models for jewelry. While working in the studio of a sculptor named Laouste, he does large decorative masks for the keystones of an arcade around a fountain at the Trocadéro Palace, which win a gold medal when exhibited under Laouste's name in the Industrial Art section of the 1878 Salon; his own *Man with a Broken Nose*, exhibited elsewhere at the same Salon under his

Carrier-Belleuse. 1882. Bronze, 23¼" high

own name, wins nothing. Also does decorative heads for the Parc de Sceaux, which are stolen as soon as set up. In Spring, 1878, he goes to Nice to collaborate with a sculptor-decorator named Cordier and does a gigantic mask of Neptune and two caryatids of sirens for the Villa Neptune on the Promenade des Anglais; also does architectural decoration for two or three months in Marseilles with an artist named Fourquet, possibly working on the Palace of Fine Arts. In 1879 goes back to work for a third time for Carrier-Belleuse, now art director of the Sèvres porcelain factory, and works there until 1882 for three francs an hour. He makes sculptural friezes for vases entitled *Nymphs and Bacchantes, The Elements, Winter, Illusions, Day* and *Night* by engraving the outlines in plaster, which are prepared for firing by another artisan, but does not attempt to learn the techniques of firing and glazing. (A co-worker, Taxile Doat, states that on one occasion he does an entire vase design in an hour, inspired by a work of Berlioz he has heard the previous evening.) One of the ceramic workers, Jules Desbois, becomes one of his most devoted and long-time collaborators, specializing in making marble and plaster versions of his figures. During these years, attempts unsuccessfully to get commissions for a monument to the Franco-Prussian War (for which *The Call to Arms*, page 68, is a sketch) and for others dedicated to Lazare Carnot, Diderot, Jean-Jacques Rousseau and General Marguerite.

1880– In Spring, 1880 finishes the full-scale plaster of
1881   *St. John the Baptist Preaching*, begun in 1878 (pages 27–33). *The Age of Bronze* receives third prize at the Salon; acquired by the State for 2,200 francs (the price of its casting in bronze), it is set up in the Luxembourg Gardens, where it remains until 1889. Is introduced by the painter

Maurice Haquette to his brother-in-law Edmond Turquet, Antonin Proust's successor as Minister of Fine Arts, and on July 17, 1880 is officially invited to design for the proposed Museum of Decorative Arts a monumental portal with sculpture reliefs (later to become known as *The Gates of Hell,* pages 35–48). Selecting as his subject Dante's *Divine Comedy,* he begins immediately to make first sketches and then plaster models for the architectural framework, drawing upon such earlier sculptures as the "Ugolino," the unfinished *Adam* and perhaps even a sketch of *The Thinker* which may have been begun in 1877. He estimates that he will complete the commission by 1884 (his most extensive work on the project actually continues throughout the 1880s); his correspondence with the Fine Arts Committee reveals that by 1881, he already knows the final scale and general format of *The Gates.* His request for funds to permit full-scale, free-standing figures of *Adam* and *Eve* to flank the portal is denied. By 1881 he is exhibiting with increasing frequency both in Paris and outside France.

1882   At the invitation of his old classmate at the Petite Ecole, Alphonse Legros, visits London, where he meets influential English writers such as Robert Louis Stevenson (to whom he later gives a marble version of *Springtime*) and William Ernest Henley, editor of the *Magazine of Art*; these men contribute greatly to his renown in England. Learns drypoint and engraving from Legros and makes about a dozen prints before 1887. In Paris, meets Mme Lynch de Morla Vicunha, wife of a Chilean diplomat, who is instrumental in introducing him to Paris society, later leading to important portrait commissions. Begins an extensive series of busts of

Mme Luisa Lynch de Morla Vicunha.
1884. Marble, 22½" high

his artist and writer friends. Upon receiving from the Government a studio in the Depôt des Marbres, erects the full-scale frame of *The Gates of Hell*. Death of his father.

1883   About this time he meets Camille Claudel, who becomes his mistress, collaborator and model (for almost fifteen years), posing for such works as *Aurora* (1885), *Thought* (1886; page 115), and *France* (1904; page 194), and making many of the small hands and feet used in his sculpture.

1884- Meets Medardo Rosso in the studio of Dalou.
1885   On June 25, 1884, writes the Fine Arts Committee that *The Gates of Hell* is sufficiently advanced for him to approach a founder to obtain a price for casting the portal. From friends in Calais, learns that the city desires to erect a monument to its six famous Burghers, who in 1347 had given themselves as hostages to the king of England in return for lifting the siege of their city; although the commission he receives calls for only one figure, that of Eustache de St. Pierre, he obtains permission to make at the same price the other five Burghers mentioned in Froissart's *Chronicles*. Submits models in 1884 and 1885, neither of which meets with the committee's full accord, and until the installation of the finished monument at Calais in June, 1895 he continues to fight a running battle regarding the interpretation, composition, base and site for *The Burghers of Calais* (pages 70–87).

1886- Begins work on a suite of pencil drawings to
1889   illustrate Baudelaire's *Flowers of Evil* and finishes twenty-seven of them by 1888, although they are not published until 1898 in a private edition by Gallimard. (His complaints concerning lack of funds and public sale for these illustrations are commented upon by Edmond de Goncourt at the end of 1887.) By 1886 has done a large sculpture of Christ (now lost, although the figure is re-used later in the group *Christ on the Cross Embraced by Mary Magdalene*). The rough, life-size models for all of the Burghers are completed by July of that year, and two years later two of the finished plasters of these figures are exhibited at the Galeries Georges Petit. A lifelong ambition to make an equestrian monument seems within realization when he is asked to submit a study for a monument to the Chilean general, Patrick Lynch; this model, sent to Chile, is lost and never enlarged as planned. Begins three years of work on the monument to Bastien-Lepage, inaugurated 1889 and the only monument actually begun and finished during the '80s. In 1887 the writer, Roger Marx, helps him to obtain a Government commission for a large marble version of *The Kiss*. The Boston sculptor, Truman H. Bartlett, makes the first of several visits to his studio, culminating in a series of ten articles that appears in 1889 and constitutes the best information on his life and work

up to that date (see bibl.). Receives the Cross of the Chevalier of the Legion of Honor in 1888; the same year, a half life-size sculpture of *The Thinker* is exhibited in Copenhagen.

1889- Exhibits his portrait engravings at the Salon des
1890   Peintres et Graveurs. All the figures for *The Burghers of Calais* are exhibited in Spring, 1889 at the Galeries Georges Petit as part of a large exhibition held jointly with Monet; this show, together with the inclusion of several of his most important works in the Exposition Universelle, contributes greatly to his reputation. Through the intercession of the painter Carrière, he is asked for the first time to be on a Salon jury. Invited by the Government to make a monument to Victor Hugo for the Pantheon; instead of the anticipated standing figure, he does one showing the author seated and surrounded by Muses. The study for this, submitted at the end of 1890, is judged ill suited to its projected location but is accepted for the Palais Royal (the marble figure of Hugo alone being finally installed there in 1909, to remain until 1939). In 1889, completes the bronze study for the Claude Lorrain monument to be erected at Nancy. *The Helmet-Maker's Wife* shown in Angers.

1891- Having received from the Société des Gens de
1892   Lettres, largely at the instigation of its president, Emile Zola, the commission for a monument to Balzac, he visits Tours and the Indre valley at the end of October, 1891, to make sketches of Balzac's home province. By February, 1892, he has

Project for "Monument to Victor Hugo." 1892. Plaster, 38¾" high completed a study of Balzac fully clothed, standing relaxed with arms folded and legs crossed, and another which greatly displeases his patrons, showing the subject as a naked fighter (page 92). On being asked again to make a standing figure of Victor Hugo for the Pantheon, this time he conceives of the author standing nude on a rock on the Isle of Guernsey, listening to the voices of sirens (this work is never completed, but a study is shown in 1893 at a banquet in Hugo's honor, and an enlarged plaster is made in 1897). Accepts the commission for a sculpture of Baudelaire but refuses to do a sepulchral monument of the poet for Montparnasse Cemetery (page 125). In response to public criticism, he somewhat modifies the horses in the base of the monument to Claude Lorrain, unveiled at Nancy in June, 1892, but later regrets having done so. François Pompon is working as his assistant at this time.

1893 Becomes president of the sculpture section of the National Society of Fine Arts, established four years earlier by a secessionist group of sculptors and painters withdrawing from the Society of French Artists and its official Salon in order to open a new Salon, with no awards and with the possibility of submitting non-juried entries. Gives Medardo Rosso a study for *The Walking Man* and receives in return Rosso's

Model for "Monument to Labor." 1894. Plaster

Little Laughing Girl; this exchange together with his letter of praise to Rosso leads to various conjectures about the latter's influence on the *Monument to Balzac* (see page 96). Writings on his work by Count Kessler help to extend his fame in Germany. *Andromeda* is shown in Chicago.

1894 Throughout the mid-'90s is constantly in poor health, suffering from influenza and depression, compounded by difficulties over the *Balzac*. The Société des Gens de Lettres deems his work "artistically insufficient" and calls one of his sketches "a colossal foetus"; fearing his death and the loss of their ten-thousand-franc investment, the Société persuades him to post this sum as insurance. Accounts of bitter quarreling among the sponsors of the *Balzac* reach the press, and the newspapers begin to be constantly filled with gossip and criticism of him. The rental of property at Meudon outside Paris offers him sanctuary as well as ideal working conditions. He begins three years of work on a model for a *Monument to Labor*; the towerlike model is eventually brought to the United States, where attempts to raise funds for the project prove unsuccessful. According to a former assistant, Victor Frisch (see bibl.), his first real one-man exhibitions are held this year in several German cities, Vienna and Prague.

Model for "Monument to Claude Lorrain." 1889. Bronze, 48⅜" high

1895 Presides over a banquet for Puvis de Chavannes, whom he greatly reveres. In June, *The Burghers of Calais* is installed on a high pedestal surrounded by a Gothic-style iron fence in the Place de Richelieu, Calais, to remain there until 1924, when it is finally installed, as he had hoped, in the square before the Town Hall. Successfully withstands the intrigues of Marquet de Vasselot to deprive him of the *Balzac* commission. Works on the model for a monument to the Argentine political hero, Domingo Sarmiento, which results only in a large stone carved base showing *Apollo Crushing the Python*, symbolizing the triumph of light over ignorance.

1896– Is visited by Prince Eugene of Norway and
1897 Sweden, one of frequent visits to be made to him by European royalty before his death; the bronze bust of Dalou and a plaster of *The Inner Voice* are exhibited in Stockholm. His drawings receive their most important publication, with a preface by Octave Mirbeau (see bibl.). Sends five plaster sculptures, among them *The Danaïd*, to the Second International Exhibition of Art (later known as the Biennale) in Venice. *The Sphinx* is shown in Chicago. Exhibits works in Geneva; gives the Musée Rath there three sculptures, among them *The Crouching Woman* (judged indecent, they are relegated to the basement).

1898 The *Monument to Balzac* is finished, probably by March, and exhibited in May at the Salon of the National Artists Society in the Hall of Machines on the Champ de Mars. The sponsoring committee, protesting that it has been given only a sketch, refuses to recognize the sculpture as finished and breaks its contract with him, but he takes no legal recourse. As a result of the tremendous clamor against the sculpture, he withdraws it to his home at Meudon, turns down private offers to purchase and cast it, and decides to keep it for himself; the work is never cast in his lifetime, and a project he conceives just before World War I of having Charles Despiau cut it in dark stone is never carried out (see pages 101–03). The *Balzac* affair, however, greatly increases the number of commissions he receives, even before his great one-man show two years later. Breaks off his relationship with Camille Claudel.

1899 According to Mme Goldscheider, his first great exhibitions are held this year in Holland and Belgium, for which Judith Cladel gives several lectures; he makes a triumphal tour of Holland. Begins monument to Puvis de Chavannes (never completed, but resulting in a bust and *The Spirit of Eternal Repose*, page 154).

1900– In conjunction with the Exposition Universelle
1901 at Paris, decides to present the first large-scale retrospective of his work; with the financial aid of his friends Mme Dorizon, M. Peytel and Gustave Kahn, he erects a temporary pavilion in Louis XVI style at the Place de l'Alma, adjacent to the exposition, in which he exhibits one hundred and seventy sculptures and drawings.

Though this costs him 160,000 francs, he sells over 200,000 francs worth of sculpture, receives orders for casts and marbles from foreign museums and collectors in Germany, the United States, England and Denmark, and is deluged with requests for portrait busts priced at 40,000 francs each. His staff of collaborators is enormously enlarged and now includes, among others, Victor Frisch, Alexandre Charpentier, the Schnegg brothers, Charles Despiau, Pompon, Jules Desbois and Antoine Bourdelle. With the two last-named, he founds an atelier, L'Académie Rodin, on the Boulevard Montparnasse. Exhibits his drypoints (*La Ronde, Bust of Bellona, Springtime*) for the first time at the Salon of the National Society of Fine Arts. *St. John the Baptist Preaching* is purchased as the result of a public subscription in England. The American, Edward Steichen, who has sought him out after his exhibition, is encouraged to photograph his sculptures in the studio at Meudon, which Steichen does in 1901 and 1902.

1902 Judith Cladel commences her work which leads to his finest biography. Beginning of his famous correspondence with Rainer Maria Rilke, who is temporarily employed as his secretary in 1906. One of his assistants, the Czech, Maratka, organizes an exhibition and triumphal reception for him in Prague. He gives one of the *Burghers* to that city in gratitude for its purchase of his *Age of Bronze*. Visits London and receives a triumphal reception from students at the Slade School of Fine Art. Begins his long association with the Rudier foundry, which is responsible for some of his finest castings in bronze.

1903 Again fêted in London. France awards him the Cravat of the Legion of Honor. On the death of Whistler is made President of the International Society of Painters, Sculptors and Engravers. Works on a proposed monument to Whistler, never completed; surviving studies for it include a plaster maquette and two marble heads of Muses.

1904– Has a major exhibition in Düsseldorf. Begins a
1905 long and disastrous liaison with the American-born Duchesse de Choiseul ("the Muse"), which results in the alienation of most of his old friends. Returns to the Government the funds advanced for *The Gates of Hell*. *The Thinker* is enlarged, is cast in bronze with funds raised through a public subscription of 15,000 francs, and on April 27, 1905 is set up in front of the Pantheon, where it remains until removed to the Court of Honor of the Musée Rodin in 1922. According to some sources, in 1905 enlarges *The Walking Man* in plaster. Purchases the ruins of the Château d'Issy, with the idea of restoring it as a museum to house his growing collection of ancient art, but because of the great expense preserves only the doorway; this is added to the pavilion from

the exposition of 1900 which has been transported to Meudon (where it now overlooks his grave).

1906 Does a series of portraits of George Bernard Shaw at Meudon (pages 125–28). Rilke serves as his secretary for about six months but through a misunderstanding is rudely dismissed; thanks to the poet's patience, understanding and unwavering admiration, the friendship is eventually resumed. Does a series of drawings, at Meudon and Marseilles, of the Cambodian dancers who have accompanied King Sisowath on a visit to France (pages 165, 167). His exhibition in Strasbourg is the first for a French sculptor to be held in Alsace-Lorraine since the Franco-Prussian War. With the painter Zuloaga, tours Madrid, Toledo, Cordova and Seville.

1907 *The Walking Man* in its enlarged scale is cast in bronze; he orders its patina to be reworked three times, by an artisan named Limet, who is instructed to give the sculpture the appearance of being a work of antiquity; the large-scale figure is exhibited at the Paris Salon. Is honored (together with Mark Twain) with a degree from Oxford University and sees his bust of William Ernest Henley installed in the crypt of St. Paul's.

1908 His attention is drawn by Rilke to the desirability and availability, as a place in which to live and work, of the Hôtel Biron, currently or previously tenanted by Rilke himself and other artists including Henri Matisse, Jean Cocteau and Isadora Duncan. He postpones buying the Hôtel Biron, hoping that the Government will purchase it as a permanent museum to house his works. Léonce Bénédite suggests that *The Gates of Hell* be placed at the rear of the unused chapel of the Seminary of St. Sulpice and additional reliefs be made to accompany it, but these proposals are not carried out. Receives visits from King Edward VII of England, and from the King of Greece who invites him to visit that country. Fifty-eight of his wash drawings are exhibited at Stieglitz's "291" Gallery in New York, as a result of his friendship with Edward Steichen, who in September comes to Meudon and photographs the *Balzac* out of doors at night (pages 104, 201). The Metropolitan Museum of Art decides to acquire a large number of his important sculptures.

1910– Beginning of publications of his views on art:
1912 article on the *Venus de Milo* in *L'Art et les Artistes*, March, 1910, and *L'Art, Entretiens réunis par Paul Gsell*, 1911 (see bibl.). Bust of the statesman Clemenceau (page 129). During these last years and until his death in 1917, he is surrounded by intrigue and jealous fighting for favor among his defenders; his problems are compounded by the decline of his mental faculties owing to advanced age, his incapacity to manage his own business affairs and his alternating blind trust

Gertrude Käsebier. *Auguste Rodin.* c. 1906–07. Platinum print

and heedless distrust. He is also plagued by forgeries and actual thefts from his studio by professed friends, and constant entanglements with the press and critics. Loyal friends such as Judith Cladel frequently help to avert disaster and keep alive the project for a museum devoted to his work. In 1911, the British Government purchases a cast of *The Burghers of Calais* to set up next to the Houses of Parliament; he goes to inspect the site, but his indecisiveness regarding the base causes disagreement. Friends in Paris purchase a bronze cast of his enlarged *Walking Man* and present it to the French Government for its embassy in the Farnese Palace, Rome; in 1912 he goes to inspect its location but is snubbed by Italian officials (though not by Italian artists), almost provoking an international incident. The French ambassador, disliking the work, has it removed as an obstacle to traffic (pages 173–74); it is later sent to Lyon. His defense in the press replying to an attack on Nijinsky's performance in *The Afternoon of a Faun* leads to another scandal; the dancer subsequently poses for him (page 143). Plans for donating his art to the nation for a museum continue to take form, and a petition is circulated among noted men of art, letters and politics; *The Call to Arms* is enlarged with the idea that it would be an important addition to this museum. Experiments with reproducing in glass his earlier heads of Hanako and Camille Claudel; also experiments about this time with ceramic and has the bust of the Burgher, Jean d'Aire, cast in this medium. The head for which Camille Claudel posed (variously called *France, Byzantine Princess* and *Empress of the Lower Nile*; page 194) is erected May 3, 1912 at Crown Point, New York, as a monument to the three-hundreth anniversary of the discovery of Lake Champlain. The Metropolitan Museum of Art officially opens its collection of his sculptures selected for purchases by Edward Robinson and Daniel Chester French, with funds provided by Thomas Fortune Ryan. About this time Kaiser Wilhelm II inquires about the possibility of having a bust modeled but is refused. Among many honors, he is at his time a member of the Académie des Beaux-Arts, a Grand Officer in the Legion of Honor, Vice-President of the National Society of Artists, and President both of the Society of Sculptors and of the International Society of Painters and Sculptors in London.

1913 His conversations with Dujardin-Beaumetz, Under-Secretary for Fine Arts, privately published (see bibl.). He offers his valuable collection of ancient art to the nation. His drawings are included in the Armory Show in New York; he engages in an unsuccessful project to make a statue of Joan of Arc, using the *Head of Sorrow,* to be sent to the United States. Supervises installation of *The Burghers* next to the Houses of Parliament in London.

1914 Publication of a collection of his articles on French cathedrals, illustrated with his own drawings (see bibl.). Shortly after the outbreak of war, he and Rose accompany Judith Cladel to England; he expresses his gratitude to that country, following a large exhibition of his art at Grosvenor House, by giving eighteen bronzes to the Victoria and Albert Museum. He is bitterly censured in the press for allowing one of his sculptures, called *Aphrodite*, to be used on the stage in Paris for a performance of Pierre Louÿs' work by that title. Suffering from poor health, he travels to southern France.

1915 While visiting in Rome is asked to make a portrait of Pope Benedict XV; after a long delay, during a second trip to Rome he is permitted three or four sittings, but the Pope is impatient with his methods and demands for more time (page 130–31).

1916 Makes a formal offer of the gift of all his work to the French Government for a Musée Rodin to be installed in the Hôtel Biron; this is finally accepted at the end of the year only after much dispute and largely with the aid of support rallied by Judith Cladel. During this year has *The Gates of Hell* assembled in plaster (according to Léonce Bénédite, first curator of the Musée Rodin); however, by the time of his death the next year they are again denuded (page 47). Suffers a stroke from overwork.

1917 At the end of January marries Rose, partly to buttress her legal rights in the event of his death; fifteen days later, she herself dies. Agrees to do a bust of King Albert of Belgium. The last work he is actually engaged upon is the final bust in a series portraying Etienne Clémentel, Minister of Commerce. Contracts pneumonia, aggravated by lack of heat, and succumbs November 17. A modest funeral service is held at Meudon; on his bier are placed his doctoral robe from Oxford, and the Knight's Cross of the Legion of Honor. He is buried next to Rose, with *The Thinker* as his headstone.

Hôtel Biron, now the Musée Rodin, Paris

SELECTED BIBLIOGRAPHY

Items marked with an asterisk list additional references

BOOKS BY AND ABOUT RODIN

Alhadeff, Albert. *Academic and Italian Sources of the Early Work of Auguste Rodin*. Unpublished thesis for Master of Arts degree, New York University, 1962 (typescript).

Baudelaire, Charles. *Les Fleurs du mal*, illustrated by Auguste Rodin. London, Limited Editions Club, 1940.

Bénédite, Léonce. *Rodin*. Paris, Levy, 1924. English translation: London, Benn, 1924.

——. *Rodin*. Maîtres de l'art moderne. Paris, Rieder, 1926.

Bourdelle, Antoine. *La Sculpture et Rodin* ... précédée de "Quatre pages de journal" par Claude Aveline. Paris, Emile-Paul, 1937.

Brieger, Lothar. *Auguste Rodin*. Ueber Kunst der Neuzeit, 9. Strasbourg, Heitz, 1903.

Bünemann, Hermann. *Auguste Rodin: Die Bürger von Calais*. Stuttgart, Reclam, 1957.

Burckhardt, Carl. *Rodin und das plastische Problem*. Basel, Schwabe [1921?].

Butler, Ruth. *Literary Aspects in the Work of Auguste Rodin*. Unpublished thesis for Master of Arts degree, New York University, 1957 (typescript).

Charbonneaux, Jean. *Les Sculptures de Rodin*. Bibliothèque Aldine des arts, 10. Paris, Hazan, 1949.

Chefs d'œuvre de Rodin. Photographs by René-Jacques, preface by Georges Lecomte. Paris, Les Publications Techniques et Artistiques, 1946.

*Ciolkowska, Muriel. *Rodin*. Little Books on Art. London, Methuen, 1912. Bibliography, pp. 160-66.

Cladel, Judith. *Auguste Rodin, l'œuvre et l'homme*. Preface by Camille Lemonnier. Brussels, Van Oest, 1908. English translation by S. K. Star: *Rodin, The Man and His Art, with leaves from his notebook*. Introduction by James Huneker. New York, Century, 1917.

——. *Rodin, sa vie glorieuse, sa vie inconnue*. Paris, Gallimard, 1936; definitive edition, Paris, Grasset, 1950. English translation by James Whitall: *Rodin*. New York, Harcourt, Brace, 1937.

Claris, Edmond. *De l'Impressionisme en sculpture*. Paris, La Nouvelle Revue, 1902. Correlates articles first published in *La Nouvelle Revue* (Paris) and *La Lectura* (Madrid), and *Der Impressionismus in der Skulptur* (Utrecht, de Vroede, 1902).

Coquiot, Gustave. *Rodin à l'Hôtel Biron et à Meudon*. Paris, Ollendorff, 1917. Report of debates in French Chamber of Deputies and Senate regarding establishment of the Musée Rodin, pp. 130-224.

——. *Le Vrai Rodin*. Paris, Tallandier, 1913.

Delteil, Loys. *Rude, Barye, Carpeaux, Rodin. Le Peintre-graveur illustré, XIXe et XXe siècles*, vol. 6. Paris, Chez l'auteur, 1910.

Les Dessins d'Auguste Rodin. Preface by Octave Mirbeau. Paris, Boussod, Manzi, Joyant, 1897. 129 plates reproducing 142 drawings in facsimile by Maison Goupil.

Dircks, Rudolf. *Auguste Rodin*, with a list of his principal works. London, Siegle, Hill, 1909.

Dujardin-Beaumetz, Henri-Charles-Etienne. *Entretiens avec Rodin*. Paris, Dupont, 1913. A microfilm of this privately printed work exists in The Museum of Modern Art Library.

*Elsen, Albert E. *Rodin's Gates of Hell*. Minneapolis, University of Minnesota, 1960. Bibliography, pp. 155-56.

Emde, Ursule. *Rilke und Rodin*. Marburg/Lahn, Kunstgeschichtliche Seminar, 1949.

Exposition de 1900: L'Oeuvre de Rodin. Prefaces by Eugène Carrière, Jean-Paul Laurens, Claude Monet, Albert Besnard. Introduction and catalogue by Arsène Alexandre. Paris, Société d'Edition Artistique, 1900.

*Frisch, Victor and Shipley, Joseph T. *Auguste Rodin, a Biography*. New York, Stokes, 1939. Includes a chronological list of Rodin's sculpture.

Gantner, Joseph. *Rodin und Michelangelo*. Vienna, Schroll, 1953.

Geissbuhler, Elizabeth Chase. *Rodin: Later Drawings*, with interpretations by Antoine Bourdelle. Boston, Beacon Press, 1963.

Goldscheider, Cécile. *Rodin, sa vie, son œuvre, son héritage*. Paris, Les Productions de Päris, 1962.

*Grappe, Georges. *Catalogue du Musée Rodin. I. Hôtel Biron. Essai de classement chronologique des œuvres d'Auguste Rodin*. 5th ed., Paris, 77, rue de Varenne, 1944. Bibliography, pp. 142-48.

Grautoff, Otto. *Auguste Rodin*. Künstler Monographien, 93. Bielefeld & Leipzig, Velhagen & Klasing, 1908.

Kahn, Gustave. *Auguste Rodin*. L'Art et le beau. Paris, 1906.

Lawton, Frederick. *The Life and Work of Auguste Rodin*. London, T. Fisher Unwin, 1906; New York, Scribners, 1907.

*Ludovici, Anthony M. *Personal Reminiscences of Auguste Rodin*. Philadelphia, Lippincott, 1926. Bibliography, p. 201.

Maillard, Léon. *Auguste Rodin, statuaire*. Etudes sur quelques artistes originaux. Paris, H. Floury, 1899.

Marx, Roger. *Auguste Rodin, céramiste*. Paris, Société de Propagation des Livres d'Art, 1907.

*Mauclair, Camille. *Auguste Rodin, L'Homme et l'œuvre*. Bibliothèque internationale de critique; lettres et arts. Paris, La Renaissance du Livre, 1918. English translation by Clementina Black: *Auguste Rodin, the Man, His Ideas, His Works*. London, Duckworth, 1905. Bibliography, pp. 128-29.

Musée du Louvre, Paris. *Rodin inconnu*. Exhibition, Dec. 1962–Jan. 1963. Catalogue by Cécile Goldscheider.

Musée Rodin, Paris. *Balzac et Rodin*. Exhibition, 1950. Catalogue by Cécile Goldscheider.

———. *Rodin, ses collaborateurs et ses amis*. Exhibition, 1957. Catalogue by Cécile Goldscheider.

National Museum of Modern Art, Tokyo. *Catalogue du Musée National d'Art Occidental*. Tokyo, 1961. Text in Japanese and French, with some titles in English. Includes 63 sculptures, 27 watercolors and drawings by Rodin.

Nostitz, H. *Rodin in Gesprächen und Briefen*. Dresden, 1949.

Pierron, V. Sander. *Rude et Rodin à Bruxelles*. Brussels, 1903.

Rilke, Rainer Maria. *Auguste Rodin*. Berlin, 1903 & Leipzig, Insel, 1913. English translation by Jessie Lemont and Hans Trausil. London, Grey Walls Press, 1946.

———. *Lettres à Rodin*. Preface by Georges Grappe. Paris, Emile-Paul, 1928–34.

———. *Rodin Nudes*. Le Ballet des Muses. Paris, Courrier Graphique, n.d.

Rodin, Auguste. *A la Vénus de Milo*. Preface by A.-H. Martine. Paris, La Jeune Parque, 1945. Reprinted from *L'Art et les Artistes*, March, 1910. English translation by Dorothy Dudley: *Venus: To the Venus of Milo*. New York, Huebsch, 1912.

———. *L'Art, Entretiens réunis par Paul Gsell*. Paris, Grasset, 1911; new edition, revised, 1951. English translation by Romilly Fedden: *Art*, London, Hodder & Stoughton, 1912. Reissued as *On Art and Artists*. Introduction by Alfred Werner. New York, Philosophical Library, 1957.

———. *Les Cathédrales de France*. Introduction by Charles Morice. Paris, Colin, 1914; 2nd edition, 1921.

Rodin inconnu: Images de Rudomine. Introduction by Marcel Aubert, commentary by Robert Gabert. Paris, Editions de l'Archipel [1950].

Rodin Museum of Philadelphia. Catalogue compiled by Fridolyn G. Watkins. Philadelphia, n.d.

Roh, Franz. *Rodin*. Bern, Scherz, 1939.

Sigogneau, Albert. *Le Tourment de Rodin*. Bordeaux, Delmas, 1933.

Story, Sommerville. *Rodin*. Phaidon Edition. Catalogue by Georges Grappe. New York, Oxford, 1939. Revised edition (without Grappe catalogue), London, Phaidon, 1961.

Sutton, Denys. *Rodin*. Penguin Series of Sculptors, edited by John Russell. London, Penguin, 1963.

Tirel, Marcelle. *Rodin intime*. Preface by Judith Cladel. Paris, Edition du Monde Nouveau, 1923. English translation by R. Francis: *The Last Years of Rodin*. London, Philpot, 1925.

Victoria and Albert Museum, London. *Catalogue of Sculpture by Auguste Rodin*, by E. R. D. Maclagan. 2nd edition, London, 1925.

Weinberg, Louis. *The Art of Rodin*. New York, Modern Library, 1918.

ARTICLES IN BOOKS AND PERIODICALS

Alloway, Lawrence. "Iconography Hunters and Maenad Wreckers," *Art International*, V, April, 1961, p. 3. A review of Albert E. Elsen's *Rodin's Gates of Hell*.

L'Art et les Artistes, XIX, no. 109, 1914, pp. 1-112. Special number devoted to Rodin, including the following articles: Octave Mirbeau, "Auguste Rodin," pp. 3-6; "Essai biographique," pp. 7-11; Paul Gsell, "En haut de la colline," pp. 13-28; Mme L. Bernardein-Sjoestedt, "L'Atelier de Rodin à Meudon," pp. 29-36; "Pensées inédites de Rodin," pp. 37-40; "Le Musée Rodin," pp. 41-44; Judith Cladel, "L'Hôtel Biron," pp. 45-48; Paul Gsell, "Chez Rodin," pp. 49-72; Francis de Miomandre, "Les Dessins de Rodin," pp. 73-84; Léonce Bénédite, "Propos sur Rodin," pp. 85-90; Auguste Rodin, "Vénus" (reprinted from issue of March, 1910), pp. 91-104; "Les Oeuvres de Rodin en France et à l'étranger" (from O. Grautoff's monograph), pp. 105-107; "Essai bibliographique," pp. 109-111.

Bartlett, Truman H. "August Rodin, Sculptor," *American Architect and Building News*, XXV, nos. 682-703, Jan. 19-June 15, 1889, pp. 27-29, 44-45, 65-66, 99-101, 112-14, 198-200, 223-25, 249-51, 260-63, 283-85. Serialized interview in ten installments.

Bénédite, Léonce. "Dante et Rodin," in *Dante: Mélanges de critique et d'érudition françaises* (Paris, Librairie Française, 1921), pp. 209-19.

Boeck, Wilhelm. "Rodins 'Höllenpforte': Ihre kunstgeschichtliche Bedeutung," *Wallraf-Richarts Jahrbuch*, XVI, 1954, pp. 161-95.

Brancusi, Constantin. "Hommage à Rodin," in exhibition catalogue, *Quatrième Salon de la Jeune Sculpture* (Paris, Gizard, 1952).

Breck, Joseph. "The Collection of Sculptures by Auguste Rodin in The Metropolitan Museum of Art," *Metropolitan Museum of Art Bulletin*, May, 1912, suppl.; reissued Aug., 1913.

Camera Work, no. 34/35, April-July 1911. Includes photographs of Rodin and his work by Edward Steichen, and the following special articles: Benjamin de Casseres, "Rodin and the Eternality of the Pagan Soul," pp. 13-14; Agnes Ernst Meyer, "Some Recollections of Rodin," pp. 15-19; "Rodin's Balzac," pp. 19-21; "Arthur Symons on Rodin's Drawings" (reprinted from *Camera Work*, no. 12, Oct. 1905), pp. 63-64.

*Cladel, Judith, "Rodin," in Bénézit, E., *Dictionnaire des peintres, sculpteurs, dessinateurs et graveurs*, new edition (Paris, Gründ, 1954), VII, pp. 299-303. Includes list of Rodin's sculptures.

Cogniat, Raymond. "Rodin," in Maillard, Robert, *Dictionary of Modern Sculpture* (New York, Tudor [1960]), pp. 254-58. Translated by Bettina Wadia from the French edition (Paris, Hazan, 1960).

Elsen, Albert E. "The Genesis of Rodin's Gates of Hell," *Magazine of Art*, XLV, March, 1952, pp. 100-19.

——. "The Humanism of Rodin and Lipchitz," *College Art Journal*, XLVII, Spring, 1958, pp. 247-65.

Fontainas, André. "Le Balzac de Rodin est offert à Paris," *Mercure de France*, CCLXXXV, 1938, pp. 286-97.

Gardner, Albert ten Eyck. "The Hand of Rodin," *Metropolitan Museum of Art Bulletin*, n.s., XV, 1956/57, pp. 200-04.

Geffroy, Gustave. "Auguste Rodin," in exhibition catalogue, *Claude Monet; Auguste Rodin* (Paris, Galerie Georges Petit, 1889).

Goldscheider, Cécile. "La Genèse d'une œuvre: le Balzac de Rodin," *Bulletin Esthétique*, LV, no. 95, 1951, pp. 201-03.

——. "La Genèse d'une œuvre: le Balzac de Rodin," *Revue des Arts*, II, March, 1952, pp. 37-44.

——. "Rodin en Belgique," *Médecine de France*, XL, 1958, pp. 17-21.

——. "Rodin: l'influence de la gravure anglaise sur le projet primitif de la 'Porte de l'Enfer'," *Bulletin de la Société de l'Histoire de l'Art Français*, 1950.

——. "Rodin et le monument de Victor Hugo," *Revue des Arts*, VI, Oct., 1956, pp. 179-84.

Grappe, Georges. "Rodin collectionneur," *Le Cousin Pons*, XI, n.s.i., Jan. 1-15, 1928, pp. 7-15.

——, Gréber, Jacques and White, Gilbert. "Musée Rodin de Philadelphie, Fondation Mastbaum," *Renaissance de l'Art Français*, IX, Nov., 1926, pp. 593-600.

*Grohmann, Will. "Rodin," in Thieme-Becker, *Allgemeines Lexikon der bildenden Künstler*, XXVIII (Leipzig, 1934), pp. 462-64.

Gsell, Paul. "Naissance d'une vocation: les premières années de Rodin," *Le Livre et ses Amis*, XI, 1946, pp. 7-10.

Lecomte, Georges. "La Statue de Balzac par Rodin: une bataille de 41 ans," in exhibition catalogue, *Balzac et Rodin* (Paris, Musée Rodin, 1950), pp. 5-8.

Lipchitz, Jacques. "About Rodin," in exhibition catalogue, *Auguste Rodin* (New York, Curt Valentin Gallery, May 4-29, 1954).

Mâle, Emile. "Rodin interprète les cathédrales de France," *Gazette des Beaux-Arts*, sér. 4, XI, 1914, pp. 372-78. A review of Rodin's *Les Cathédrales de France*.

Nathanson, Thadée. "Auguste Rodin," *Arts de France*, VII, 1946, pp. 24-34.

Paris, W. Francklyn. "Rodin as a Symbolist," *International Studio*, XLIX, April, 1913, pp. xlii-lv.

La Plume, XII, Paris, 1900. Special numbers devoted to Rodin, including articles by Octave Mirbeau, Stuart Merrill, Camille Mauclair, Gustave Kahn, Charles Morice, Gustave Geffroy, Gustave Coquiot, Albert Mockel, Arthur Symons, Roger Marx, Frank Harris, André Veidaux, André Fontainas, Léon Riotor, Rambosson, Louis Sauty, André Mellerio, Raymond Bouyer, Henri Frantz, May Armand Blanc, Karl Boès.

Rilke, Rainer Maria. "Le Balzac de Rodin," *Pour l'Art*, no. 33, 1953, pp. 9-10.

Rod, Edouard. "L'Atelier de M. Rodin," *Gazette des Beaux-Arts*, sér. 3, XIX, May, 1898, pp. 419-30.

"Rodin's Balzac in the Museum of Modern Art, New York," *Art Quarterly*, XVIII, no. 4, 1955, pp. 419-21.

Schmoll, J. A. gen. Eisenwerth. "Zur Genesis des Torso-Motivs und zur Deutung des fragmentarischen Stils bei Rodin," *Das Unvollendete als Künstlerische Form*, ein Symposion, herausgegeben von J. A. Schmoll gen. Eisenwerth (Berne & Munich, Francke, 1959).

Shaw, George Bernard. "Rodin," *Annales Politiques Littéraires* (Paris), Dec. 2, 1932.

——. "Rodin," *Gil Blas* (Paris), November 24, 1912.

Simmel, Georg. "L'Oeuvre de Rodin comme expression de l'esprit moderne," in *Mélanges de philosophie relativiste* (Paris, Alcan, 1912). Translated by Ben Rubi from the German (Leipzig, 1900).

Smiley, Charles Newton. "Rodin in the Metropolitan Museum," *Art and Archaeology*, III, Feb., 1916, pp. 107-09; March, 1916, pp. 165-71.

Steinberg, Leo. "Introduction," in exhibition catalogue, *Rodin, Sculptures and Drawings* (New York, Charles E. Slatkin Galleries, 1963); catalogue notes by Cécile Goldscheider.

——. "Sculpture since Rodin," *Art Digest*, XXVII, Aug., 1953, pp. 22-23. A review of Andrew Carnduff Ritchie, *Sculpture of the Twentieth Century*, New York, Museum of Modern Art, 1952.

Tyler, Parker. "Rodin and Freud: Masters of Ambivalence," *Art News*, LIV, March, 1955, pp. 38-41, 63-64.

In addition to the above, the files of news letters and clippings in the Musée Rodin, the Bernard Prost collection in the Cabinet des Estampes of the Bibliothèque Nationale (*Notes sur les artistes modernes, découpures d'articles de journaux classés par noms d'artistes*, 9 vols.), and the typescript of Rodin's letters and news articles about him, translated into English, in the Free Library of Philadelphia (of which a microfilm exists in The Museum of Modern Art Library), have also been consulted.

LIST OF ILLUSTRATIONS

All works are by Rodin unless otherwise indicated. The dates given for each work generally refer to the original version in plaster; those relating to the chapter "Some Offspring of The Gates of Hell" (pages 49–66) refer to the work's first appearance in the portal, rather than to its isolation as an independent sculpture. When two dates are given, the first designates the original plaster, the second the date of the first casting in bronze (which, however, may not be that of the cast illustrated). According to Mme Cécile Goldscheider, Director of the Musée Rodin, Paris, Rodin's accounts have not been preserved, and the date of the first casting generally cannot be determined; researches now in progress may yield further information.

In dimensions, height precedes width and depth. References are given to Georges Grappe's catalogue of the Musée Rodin (1944 edition) whenever the works here reproduced are listed in that catalogue (although not necessarily in the same medium or scale of enlargement).

Where no photographers' credits are given, the illustrations are from photographs provided by the respective collections. All those from The Rodin Museum, Philadelphia (created by the gifts of the late Jules E. Mastbaum) are reproduced by courtesy of the Commissioners of Fairmount Park and the Philadelphia Museum of Art. A list of photographers is given on page 223.

PAGE	TITLE, DATE, MEDIUM, DIMENSIONS, COLLECTION	GRAPPE NO.	PHOTOGRAPHER
79	*Torso: Study for the Burgher Pierre de Wiessant.* 1885-86? Bronze, 74⅞″ high. The Minneapolis Institute of Arts, Minneapolis	—	—
80	*The Mighty Hand (Grande Main Crispée).* 1884-86. Bronze, 18¼″ high. Jules E. Mastbaum Collection (Courtesy Mrs. Jefferson Dickson, New York)	—	Soichi Sunami
81	*Composition of Heads and Hands from "The Burghers of Calais."* Plaster, 8½″ high x 11″ long x 9¼″ deep. The Rodin Museum, Philadelphia	—	—
84, 85	*The Burghers of Calais.* 1884-86. Bronze (1895; this cast c. 1925-28), 85″ high including base 91¼″ long x 70⅜″ deep x 6½″ high. The Rodin Museum, Philadelphia	167	John Szarkowski
86	Alberto Giacometti. *City Square.* 1948. Bronze, 8½″ high (base 25⅜″ long x 17¼″ deep). The Museum of Modern Art, New York (Purchase)	—	Soichi Sunami
87	*Jean de Fiennes* (detail of *The Burghers of Calais*). Musée Rodin, Paris	—	Louis-Frédéric
88	*Monument to Balzac.* 1897. Bronze (by 1930; this cast 1954), 111″ high. The Museum of Modern Art, New York (presented in Memory of Curt Valentin by His Friends)	289	Soichi Sunami
	Studies for the "Monument to Balzac." 1892-95:		
90	*Head.* Plaster, 17″ high. Musée Rodin, Paris	—	—
90	*Head.* Terra cotta and plaster, 8¼″ high. Musée Rodin, Paris	—	—
90	*Head.* Terra cotta, 9½″ high. The Metropolitan Museum of Art, New York (Rogers Fund, 1912)	—	—
91	*Head.* Wax, 8¼″ high. Collection Mme Marcel Pollak, Paris	—	© Leni Iselin
91	*Head.* Plaster, 7½″ high. Collection Margit Chanin, Ltd., New York	—	—
92	*Balzac, Clothed.* Plaster, 23⅝″ high. Musée Rodin, Paris	—	—
92	*Balzac, Nude.* 1893. Bronze, 17¾″ high. Musée Rodin, Paris	—	Adelys
94	*Bust of Balzac.* Bronze, 18½″ high. The Joseph H. Hirshhorn Collection, New York	—	Courtesy The Solomon R. Guggenheim Museum
95	*Balzac, Nude.* Bronze (this cast 1957), 50¼″ high. Collection Mr. and Mrs. Alan Wurtzburger, Pikesville, Maryland (Courtesy The Baltimore Museum of Art)	267	Leonard L. Greif, Jr.
96	*Study for Balzac's Robe.* Terra cotta, 13¾″ high. Musée Rodin, Meudon	—	Adelys
97	*Headless Nude Torso.* Plaster, 37¾″ high. Musée Rodin, Paris	—	Bernès-Marouteau
98	*Monument to Balzac: Final Small-Scale Study.* 1897. Plaster, 41¾″ high. Musée Rodin, Meudon	—	Bernès-Marouteau
99	*Monument to Balzac: Final Enlarged Version.* 1897. Plaster, 118″ high. Musée Rodin, Meudon	289	Archives Photographiques
100	*Monument to Balzac.* 1897. Bronze (by 1930; this cast 1954). 111″ high. The Museum of Modern Art, New York (Presented in Memory of Curt Valentin by His Friends)	289	Lee Boltin
103	*Seal Posed as Balzac.* 1898? Plaster, 9¼″ high. The Rodin Museum, Philadelphia	—	—
104	Edward Steichen. "*Balzac*" — *The Silhouette, 4 a.m.* Meudon, 1908. Pigment print. The Metropolitan Museum of Art (Gift of Alfred Stieglitz)	—	Steichen
106	*The Man with the Broken Nose.* 1863-64. Bronze, 9½″ high. Musée Rodin, Paris	8	Schneider-Lengyel
108	*Jean-Baptiste Rodin, the Artist's Father.* 1860. Gilded bronze (1918), 16⅛″ high. Musée Rodin, Paris	3	Schneider-Lengyel
108	*Père Pierre-Julien Eymard.* 1863. Bronze (after 1907), 23½″ high. The Rodin Museum, Philadelphia	7	—
110	*The Little Man with the Broken Nose.* 1882. Bronze, 5″ high. The California Palace of the Legion of Honor, San Francisco (Spreckels Collection)	78	Proctor Jones
112	*Mignon (Rose Beuret).* 1870. Plaster, 15¾″ high. Musée Rodin, Paris	14	Archives Photographiques
113	*Miss Eve Fairfax.* c. 1905. Marble, 21⅝″ high. Musée Rodin, Paris	348	—

221

COLOR PLATES

LIST OF PHOTOGRAPHERS

FRANCE *Calais:* Jean·Boutté. *Paris:* Adelys; Archives Photographiques de la Caisse Nationale des Monuments Historiques; Bernès-Marouteau; Bulloz; Giraudon; Leni Iselin; Louis-Frédéric; F. Rousseaux; Jeromir Stephany; André Vigneali; Vizzavona

ITALY *Florence:* Brogi. *Rome:* Anderson

SWITZERLAND: *Buochs:* Leonard von Matt

WEST GERMANY *Munich:* Schneider-Lengyel

U.S.A. *Baltimore, Md.:* Leonard L. Greif, Jr. *Bloomington, Ind.:* Albert E. Elsen. *Boston, Mass.:* Barney Burstein; Steven Trefonides. *New York, N.Y.:* Oliver Baker Associates; Lee Boltin; Brenwasser; Frank Lerner; Elisabeth C. Loewenstein; O. E. Nelson; R. Peter Petersen; John D. Schiff; Studly; Soichi Sunami; John Szarkowski. *Oberlin, O.:* A. E. Princehorn. *Port Chester, N.Y.:* Brigadier Studios. *San Francisco, Calif.:* Pirkle Jones; Proctor Jones. *West Redding, Conn.:* Edward Steichen